Having the Last
SAY

Having the Last SAY

Alan Gelb

CAPTURING YOUR LEGACY
IN ONE SMALL STORY

JEREMY P. TARCHER/PENGUIN
an imprint of Penguin Random House
New York

JEREMY P. TARCHER/PENGUIN
An imprint of Penguin Random House LLC
375 Hudson Street
New York, New York 10014

Stories by Anne B. Rosen, Alice Swersey, Steven Kerner, Lydia Kukoff,
Daniel Wise, Barbara Lax, Tamar Cole, and "Nathalie" used with permission.

Most Tarcher/Penguin books are available at special quantity discounts for bulk
purchase for sales promotions, premiums, fund-raising, and educational needs.
Special books or book excerpts also can be created to fit specific needs.
For details, write: SpecialMarkets@penguinrandomhouse.com.

Library of Congress Cataloging-in-Publication Data

Gelb, Alan.
Having the last say : capturing your legacy in one small story / Alan Gelb.
                    p.   cm.
Includes index.
ISBN 978-0-399-17487-2
1. Autobiography—Authorship.   2. Storytelling.   3. Narration (Rhetoric).
4. Biography as a literary form.   I. Title.
CT25.G45   2015   2015002866
808.06'692—dc23

Printed in the United States of America
1 3 5 7 9 10 8 6 4 2

Book design by Ellen Cipriano

For my grandchildren,

Ruben and Nina,

who have been having their "first says."

CONTENTS

PREFACE

I was born in 1950, which means that I am not getting any younger.

Like so many of my fellow baby boomers, my body feels its years when I rise in the morning and, as the comedians say, there is less hair on my head and more in my ears. Recently, I lost my parents, who died at the ages of ninety and ninety-one, and welcomed two grandchildren; these events have catapulted me into a new stage of life in which the march of time is finally undeniable. Like so many of my contemporaries, I am trying to do the work that needs to be done at this point—looking toward the future with as much fortitude as I can muster and looking toward the past in order to gain insight into what my life has been about.

Often these days, when my wife and I get together with friends, the subject comes around to how different things are now that we are no longer . . . how shall we say it? "young." We joke about going to restaurants where we are decades older than everyone else and can't hear each other for all the background noise. Conversation often touches on things like acid reflux, knee replacements, and long-term-care insurance. Still young enough to be somewhat stunned by such developments, we joke—and then we don't. Having come into maturity at a time of women's and men's consciousness groups, we think about forming such a group to discuss issues of aging—and then we don't. On some level, we wish to share our thoughts, concerns, and fears about growing older, but we don't have the right vehicle for doing so. This seems a pity, as we still have sharp mental acuity and now we even have some wisdom to go along with it.

We are also confronting another challenging reality at this time of life: more and more, we are attending the funerals of close friends. That is heartbreaking but, as affecting as it is to say good-bye to those you care about, I must confess that I have sat through some of these services with what you might call a critical eye. While I am moved by the memories that are shared, on more than one occasion I have felt that I was missing the presence of the person being eulogized. Even though it makes sense to miss the presence of a person at his or her own funeral—after all, in a purely corporeal sense, they are no longer with us—I still felt that I wanted to hear that person one last time. I wanted that person to be in the room with us, and I wanted him or her to *have the last say*.

Now, I realize that it takes a certain kind of audacity to

critique a funeral, but I've spent a great deal of time over the last decade helping people construct narratives that serve as a form of life review and I can't help but feel that most of us are capable of expressing our thoughts through the written word. I believe that many of us would like to have that last say and might seize upon the opportunity if we understood what it was all about. It is the goal of this slim book to introduce this idea to readers and to motivate them to take on this assignment and succeed with it.

In 2008, I published another slim volume entitled *Conquering the College Admissions Essay in 10 Steps.* In the years since its publication, my book has helped thousands of 17- and 18-year-olds learn how to approach that daunting assignment with confidence and direction. Its focus is on creating a powerful narrative in a short space, operating from the conviction that a powerful narrative—that is, a strong story—is what will lodge in the mind of the over-burdened admissions counselor. Working with students has shown me just how effective the average person can be at crafting a powerful narrative—as long as he or she under-stands that form.

With this in mind, I began to think that there was really no reason why people in the third act of their lives could not match the grace, power, and articulation that my high school students achieve. Yes, there is less of an exter-nal motivation to do such work—the lack of a pressing deadline—but perhaps more of an internal motivation (the approach of the Ultimate Deadline). And let me point out that most baby boomers I know have never met a form of self-expression they didn't like.

I was also convinced that the strategies I had developed over the years that have helped young people effectively express themselves could be successfully adapted to the purposes of older folks. The process of exploration and expression would really be the same; the only difference is that baby boomers are working with a much larger canvas.

I began to conceive of this third-act "assignment" as a short piece, some 500 to 1,000 words, so that the average person, if asked to, could deliver it orally with some measure of ease. In that short space, it should manage to capture the essence of the writer and convey or impart some kind of ethic or value that the writer wishes to share. In this sense, it would be akin to the ethical wills that have been an element in Jewish life since biblical times and that have stirred renewed interest among contemporary Jews who are looking to traditions that can confer more meaning in their lives. These ethical wills have served as documents whose purpose is to pass values from one generation to another. While I find these ethical wills to be worthwhile and often historically interesting, I do not think that they are especially interesting to read. This is why I felt it would make sense to try to use the narrative, a universally engaging mode of communication, to bring another dimension to what the ethical will seeks to do. In other words, it seemed ingenious to use a compelling story to convey or impart a value rather than doing so by some legalistic document that comes with no attendant reading/listening pleasure.

I recruited a diverse group of mature adults to participate in my experiment—some I knew, some I didn't, but few would identify themselves as seasoned writers—and I asked them to create "legacies" in the form of small stories ("small" only in the sense of word count, not in terms of impact). Ultimately, if the writer so desired, these stories could be shared with family members, friends, and other loved ones—or even read at a memorial service. If the writer wished to keep the last say private, then so be it. There is still a significant benefit to be had simply in the creation of these pieces because the act of writing can go a long way toward helping people gain greater clarity about their life experiences. Since this was very much a brand-new idea, I was curious, and a bit nervous, to see if my recruits would receive it as macabre, but, in fact, the reception was quite the opposite. Almost everyone instinctively understood what I was talking about and was eager to give it a try.

We started out by mimicking an exercise I use with my 17- and 18-year-olds, in which I ask them to respond to 25 or so exploratory questions. Interestingly, many of the questions that I posed to my test group were the same as those I give to the teenagers. As soon as the writers completed this exercise, I went over their answers with them and we nailed down a writing topic. Then they went to work, producing drafts that I commented on. I can honestly say that I was amazed by the candor and expressiveness of these writers, who clearly welcomed this opportunity to review their lives. They were able to pluck out a moment that stood for something that was important to them, and they wrote stories that were meaningful to others, both in the here and now and potentially as keepsakes for future generations.

Having the Last Say offers this same opportunity to anyone who wants to capture his or her legacy in one small story. The key is to understand the narrative form and engage in a level of reflection that you may never have attempted before. As you move along this path, you will find lots of general writing tips concerning point of view, tone, and so forth.

I believe that you will find the experience to be stimulating and ultimately rewarding—both for you and for those around you. And, unlike my high school writers who are facing so much pressure with their college admissions, you can afford to approach this writing challenge with much less anxiety. After all, there really is nothing to lose and so much to gain. In other words, this is an experience to savor and enjoy at this reflective time of life in which we find ourselves.

INTRODUCTION

Thirteen years ago, I helped found a synagogue in my small town in upstate New York. Historically, there had never been enough Jews in this rural location to warrant one, but demographic changes were under way and, with the increase in the Jewish population, the time for a synagogue had arrived.

Growing any kind of organization from square one is a story of its own—indeed, a saga—but I'm not going to go into that here. Let me just say that in building up this spiritual community, those of us who were involved took on tasks and responsibilities that were new to us. I, for one, had a truly sketchy Jewish background, but that didn't stop me from becoming a synagogue president . . . or a seller of cemetery plots.

Yes, you read that right. One initiative that our congregation took on was to establish a Jewish section of the municipal cemetery in town, and I volunteered to become the point person with regard to purchasing plots. Years later, I knew I had passed a certain threshold on my life's journey when I called a party that had expressed interest in making such a purchase and the elderly gentleman who answered the phone shouted out to his wife, "Gloria! It's the Cemetery!"

As a writer, I strongly subscribe to the philosophy that you can learn about life from doing almost anything as long as you pay sufficient attention while you're doing it, and one of the things I've learned about selling cemetery plots is that very few people are prepared for the stuff that happens in life's third act. They place at arm's length such issues as living wills, health care proxies, and, yes, cemetery plots. On multiple occasions, I have found myself working with a family in which a death has occurred and no burial arrangements were in place. And these were not situations that involved accidents or other violent upheavals. These were situations involving older individuals with manifold vulnerabilities who had chosen, for whatever reason, not to go down the path of preparation and prudence.

Now, mind you, I say all this without judgment. Denial, after all, can be such a useful and seductive tool, and few of us are immune to its charms. But denial comes with a price. A few years ago a cousin of mine died at the age of 65. He had a grave disease and went into the hospital for a treatment that came with an alarming mortality rate. Sadly, he died during that treatment.

As it turned out, my cousin entered into this treatment without first arranging for a cemetery plot. Fortunately, when he died, his friends and community were able to take care of things, but perhaps more significant, he also entered treatment without first having had some important conversations with his wife. In the years that followed his death, his wife felt acute loss over all the things that were left unsaid. Plans, feelings, dreams, regrets, hopes, fears—too much, she felt, had been left to the imagination. The process of review had been insufficient and the lack of it was painful.

LIFE REVIEW

As a generation, we baby boomers have traditionally held ourselves in high regard. After all, we gave the world Woodstock and, on some level, have always believed that what we had to say was truly important. We were raised in an idealized America, suffused with postwar optimism. Our parents, coached by Dr. Spock, promised us that we would lead happy, healthy, and productive lives, as we worked for companies that took care of us, enjoyed dental health and resistance to polio, and saw the USA in our Chevrolets. (Of course, in timely fashion, that optimism was tempered by the Cold War, the Vietnam War, Watergate, and, most recently, the economic downturn.)

For the most part, our mammoth group of nearly 75 million people who make up close to 40 percent of the nation's population has been largely invested in holding age at bay, giving way to such phenomena as *boomeritis*, which is defined as injuries to older amateur athletes. (Guilty as charged, I admit, after a herniated L4 and two bouts of sciatica.) At a certain point, however, there are no joints left to replace, age catches up, and the time for reflection is upon us. This is when the process of life review starts to feel like time well spent.

Life review, in some form or another, seems to be a universal, cross-cultural activity, sometimes formalized, often not. The work can take place on paper, in the context of formal group discussions, in conversations with friends and loved ones, or within a person's own head.

Erik Erikson, the psychoanalyst and developmental psychologist best known for his theory of psychosocial development, identified eight stages of development, each with a "virtue" that represents a favorable outcome for that stage. For instance, he cited basic trust as the virtue that should come out of the first stage of life (infancy to one year). The last stage of life, as Erikson identified it, covers the age of 65 onward. During that time, people look back on their lives and, depending on how those have progressed, will either feel a sense of integrity and accomplishment or not. The virtue that you want to come away with at this last stage of life is ego integrity—that is, an acceptance of self—and the process of life review can be enormously helpful in terms of achieving that.

However it is accomplished, life review involves organizing your memories in ways that are meaningful, thus combating the anxiety and chaos that can often take over in this last stage of life. Life review involves reflecting on the people, actions, and developmental milestones that have helped shape your life. It is work that can be alternately exhausting, exhilarating, sad, and joyful . . . or all of those things at the same time. And, of course, it doesn't have to take place only in the last stage of life. Typically, that's when it does occur, but no one is stopping you from doing life review at any age. As I said at the beginning, the high school students I work with are engaged in serious life review when they work on their college admissions essays. They just have a lot less life to review than we older folks do.

Many thousands of Americans are actively and thoughtfully pursuing memoir writing and journaling—two avenues of expression that are ideal for life review. I have found from my own experience, however, that these activities essentially appeal to people who have a well-established relationship with the written word. For such individuals, writing in journals does not feel like a big hurdle. With this book, however, I am looking to engage not only those who like to write but also those who have no significant history with writing or confidence in their abilities. To those folks, I say leave your preconceptions at the door because I believe that anyone can achieve expression through writing and can craft a valuable legacy in the form of one small story.

The high school students I work with are able to do just that. Many of them are far removed from the humanities; they are aspiring scientists, engineers, or mathematicians who may not have an especially easy relationship with the written word. But when it comes to writing their college admissions essays, they rise magnificently to the occasion. Why? Not because they are extraordinarily sensitive or insightful or dedicated (though they're pretty darned good, for the most part, in those departments) but because they *understand the narrative.*

NARRATIVES

We will be discussing the narrative in the upcoming chapter, so I don't want to show my hand here. I just want to say that as a form, the narrative comes with a prescribed structure. When you understand that structure—which you will by the end of the next chapter—then you can begin to work effectively with that form.

The narrative has been around since the dawn of human history. Sitting by the fire, cave dwellers passed their nights not with Letterman but with stories—that is, narratives. Some cave dwellers were particularly gifted at presenting narratives about the day's events—the escape from the saber-toothed tiger, the close encounter with the woolly mammoth—and so they captured the attention of their peers and became popular. After all, everyone loves a good story—and just about anyone can tell a good story.

What I have found is that when the average person understands the elements of a narrative, he or she can usually become a skilled storyteller, if only for a one-shot experience. The 17- and 18-year-olds I work with tell stories about their parents and grandparents and brothers and sisters, about their frustrations and their triumphs over adversity, about the silly things that happen to them and the passion they feel for rowing or the oboe or making popcorn. Once they understand the elements that comprise a powerful narrative, these kids tell stories that I often find unforgettable. Years after I've finished working with them, after they've gone on with their lives, graduating from college and making their way in the world, some image or detail or event from their stories will come back to me and I will feel like I am visiting with them.

ETHICAL WILLS

As I started to say a few pages ago, in the course of my Jewish journey I became aware of the practice within our tradition of writing ethical wills. The point of the ethical will was to pass values from one generation to the next, and the basis for this practice can be traced all the way back to Genesis. When they were on their deathbeds, figures like Isaac and Jacob gathered their children about them and made their wishes and values known.

The early rabbis instructed their followers to use ethical wills to convey the teachings of the Jewish tradition from generation to generation, and, over time, these wills, which were originally transmitted orally, became written documents, generally conveyed in the form of letters. Today, the ethical will has been adopted by wholly nonsectarian segments of the general public. It is used as a tool in estate planning, in health care, and as a spiritual healing tool. In his book *Healthy Aging: A Lifelong Guide to Your Physical and Spiritual Well-Being*, wellness guru Dr. Andrew Weil promotes the ethical will as "a gift of spiritual health" whose main importance is "what it gives the writer in the midst of life."

Although I have great respect for a tradition that precedes me by millennia, I have said that I don't find ethical wills to be a very engaging literary form. When I read them—even those of real historic interest—I do tend to glaze over a bit, as I am apt to do around any legal document. Ethical wills may contain content that is moving, insightful, brave, and tender—but they don't really work as pieces of writing for me. And so, I began to think about how to take that form and move it to another level: the level of *storytelling*.

TELL ME A STORY

Think about the power of stories in your life. When you were a kid, you sat around the kitchen table and listened to your grandmother or grandfather reminisce about life on the farm/in the mines/in the bayous/in the shtetl. You were captivated and you *learned*. You learned what it meant to work hard (milking those cows before the sun rose), to persevere (selling those magazine subscriptions), to carry on family traditions (baking the *pfeffernüsse* at Christmas), and more.

Just as we all benefited from hearing such stories as children, so can our stories benefit our adult children and other loved ones. In fact, they are the gifts that keep on giving. It is so important to share our mythic family stories—encountering a rabid dog on the paper route; the time the twister blew up the barn; going on a union march with Grandma. These stories, however, are most often transmitted orally and, as with all myths, they tend to become codified as time goes on. On the one hand, this is comforting—we know what to expect—but, on the other hand, a certain complexity or depth is often missing.

In an interesting piece called "The Stories That Bind

Us," published in the *New York Times* in March 2013, author Bruce Feiler describes the pressures that typically afflict modern families. He states, "The single most important thing you can do for your family may be the simplest of all: develop a strong family narrative." Feiler goes on to discuss the work of psychologist Marshall Duke, who, in the mid-1990s, was asked to help explore myth and ritual in American families. Duke and his colleague, Robyn Fivush, developed a measure called the "Do You Know?" scale, which asked children to answer a series of questions, such as "Do you know where your parents met?" or "Do you know about an illness or something really terrible that happened in your family?" or "Do you know the story of your birth?"

The findings of this study were quite surprising. The more children knew about their family histories, the stronger their sense of control over their lives and the higher their self-esteem. Indeed, the "Do You Know?" scale turned out to be the single best predictor of children's emotional health and happiness.

The stories that you will read in this book portray the *inner lives* of their authors. These stories are complex and profound and even revelatory. And, accordingly, they become very special gifts. Because isn't it amazing how we share our lives with people without necessarily knowing what goes on inside of them? When people put their inner lives out there in the form of narratives, then the special gift is delivered in ways that can astonish. For one's life partner or one's children or close friends, the sharing of such revelations can do much to make a relationship grow— even when the authors of these revelations are no longer walking beside us.

CONFESSIONAL WRITING

Confessional writing has, of late, gotten quite bad press. The Internet has become a vast repository for what are often highly undisciplined outpourings of personal information that can feel more like exhibitionism than anything else. These outpourings are frequently met by a chorus of comments charging TMI (Too Much Information, for those uninitiated in Internet lingo). All together, this creates an atmosphere that would make anyone question the merits of putting yourself out there.

In fact, however, confessional writing is an ancient form of expression in which the writer explores the way he or she has lived life. We think, for instance, of Saint Augustine's *Confessions*, often regarded as the first autobiography to come out of Western Europe. In it, Augustine recounted the events of his life and, in a manner that was revolutionary for its time, plumbed the meaning and significance of those events. A famous interlude in *Confessions* relates Augustine's theft of some pears. Let's look at that section:

> There was a pear tree close to our own vineyard, heavily laden with fruit, which was not tempting either for its color or for its flavor. Late one night—having prolonged our games in the streets until then, as our bad habit was—a group of young scoundrels, and I among them, went to shake and rob this tree. We carried off a huge load of pears, not to eat ourselves, but to dump out to the hogs, after barely tasting some of them ourselves. Doing this pleased us all the more because it was forbidden. Such was my heart, O God, such was my heart—which thou didst pity even in that bottomless pit. Behold, now let my heart confess to thee what it was seeking there, when I was being gratuitously wanton, having no inducement to evil but the evil itself. It was foul, and I loved it. I loved my own undoing. I loved my error—not that for which I erred but the error itself. A depraved soul, falling away from security in thee to destruction in itself, seeking nothing from the shameful deed but shame itself.

This was written sometime between AD 397 and AD 398. In other words, more than 1,600 years ago—and yet there is an almost modern sensibility to the author's probing of his inner life.

In a certain sense, the narrative or narratives you will write that are inspired by this book are bound to have a confessional aspect to them. This is your opportunity to explore vulnerabilities, conflict, inhibitions, and errors. And why would I want to do that? you ask. Because that is precisely the stuff of life review. But don't worry—life review need not be exclusively dark and stormy. It can just as easily be a look back at what has been rewarding, satisfying, and gratifying—relationships; work; experiencing joyful heights through travel, the arts, physical feats, or whatever. What is confessional is the act of making your inner life public—and therein lies the gift, for it can be extraordinarily powerful for those who have known and loved you to also know that you struggled, that you wrestled with vulnerabilities and regrets, and that you confronted the difficulties of the human experience as bravely and as best as you could.

IN PRAISE OF LIFE

As I mentioned at the beginning, when I started thinking about these narratives, I also found myself thinking about what it would be like to write one's own eulogy. After all, think about how special it would be to be privy to an assessment of one's place in the scheme of things. Mark Twain nailed it when he wrote about the apparent demise of Tom Sawyer and Huck Finn and the service that followed:

> As the service proceeded, the clergyman drew such pictures of the graces, the winning ways, and the rare promise of the lost lads that every soul there, thinking he recognized these pictures, felt a pang in remembering that he had persistently blinded himself to them always before and had as persistently seen only faults and flaws in the poor boys. The minister related many a touching incident in the lives of the departed, too, which illustrated their sweet, generous natures, and the people could easily see, now, how noble and beautiful those episodes were, and remembered with grief that at the time they occurred they had seemed rank rascalities, well deserving of the cowhide. The congregation became more and more moved, as the pathetic tale went on, till at last the whole company broke down and joined the weeping mourners in a chorus of anguished sobs, the preacher himself giving way to his feelings, and crying in the pulpit.
>
> There was a rustle in the gallery, which nobody noticed; a moment later the church door creaked; the minister raised his streaming eyes above his handkerchief, and stood transfixed!
>
> First one and then another pair of eyes followed the minister's, and then almost with one impulse the con-

gregation rose and stared while the three dead boys came marching up the aisle, Tom in the lead, Joe next, and Huck, a ruin of drooping rags, sneaking sheepishly in the rear! They had been hid in the unused gallery listening to their own funeral sermon!

A great narrative sequence, to be sure, but the more salient point is that the exercise you are about to engage in is a little bit like attending your own funeral and hearing your own eulogy, with the added bonus that your eulogy is something written by you yourself.

The word *eulogy* comes from the Greek εὐλογία (eulogia) for "praise." Those who eulogize say loving things about those who have departed, as in the "sweet, generous natures" of Tom and Huck, per above. Of course, Tom and Huck were absolutely not sweet and generous and so the minister's eulogy turned out to be a hollow thing. I suppose this is one of the reasons why I sometimes chafe at a funeral when I hear things that do not feel consistent with the reality of the person I have known. Eulogies tend to idealize people rather than reflect their true humanity in all its messiness—flaws and quirks and all. That's fine, but your "eulogy"—that "last say" that we are talking about—is an act of praise, as I see it. In your very short story, you will convey something about life, something you have learned, that has been profoundly meaningful for you. In doing so, you will help the people in your world understand that life, for all its difficulties and complexities, is worth living. In this sense, your piece will become an act of praise for the life you have led, imperfect as it may have been, and you will have done at least some of the work that gets you to that place of ego integrity that Erik Erikson describes.

And now it's time to move on to the actual work. What is a narrative? How does it function? And how can you get started?

CHAPTER 1

Understanding the Narrative

You've heard a lot of stories in your life, I'm sure, and you've been around a lot of storytellers. You know who tells a good story and who falls short of the mark. And I'm sure you have many good stories within you. After all, it's hard to go through life without amassing one's share of true tales and ripping yarns.

Keep in mind, however, that there can be a significant gap between thinking that you have a good story and knowing how to tell it. Soon enough, we will get into the business of looking back over our lives and identifying those stories that are waiting to be told. But first it's important that we examine the *form* of the narrative, because in order to tell a good story, we have to recognize its elements.

GATHER AROUND

OK, people. Ready for your story? Let's begin.

Last Saturday, I set out to do errands. I had the usual long list: dry cleaner, Trader Joe's, Home Depot, liquor store. Red, white, or rosé? We were having moussaka for dinner. I wasn't sure what went best with that, so I'd have to inquire.

Are you with me? So far, so good? Can't wait to hear more? No? Hmmm. Wonder why. Well, let's keep going.

I stopped to get gas and picked up some Frontline at PetSmart. Then I went to the post office to buy some stamps. Then I headed home, taking the shortcut down Old Route 23, which even on a Saturday had hardly any traffic.

Better? *No?* Jeez—tough room. OK, I'll keep trying. Taking it from the top:

Last Saturday, I set out to do my errands. I had the usual long list: dry cleaner, Trader Joe's, Home Depot, liquor store. Red, white, or rosé? We were having moussaka for dinner. I wasn't sure what went best with that, so I'd have to inquire. I stopped to get gas and picked up some Frontline at PetSmart. Then I went to the post office to buy some stamps. Then I headed home, taking the shortcut down Old Route 23, which even on a Saturday had hardly any traffic. As I headed down the road, singing along to Springsteen, I heard an ominous *thwack-thwack-thwack*. With the car rattling and shuddering, I realized I had a flat.

Ahhh. Now we've got ourselves a story, yes? But what happened to make it better? The answer is *something*. Something happened. The tire went flat, Conflict reared its delicious head, and the story started to come to life.

From the moment the tire goes flat, anything can happen. We might, for instance, confront a host of further complications: the jack is missing, the spare tire needs air, the cell phone is out of its charge. It's just that kind of day.

Or how about this scenario? I get out of the car, roll up my sleeves, and get to work. It's been years since I changed a flat, but there is real pleasure to be had in remembering what goes where and in getting the job done. Until I feel a twinge in my back. More Conflict.

Or maybe it goes in this direction: I call the emergency road service, but it soon becomes obvious that the call center is located in India. As I try to explain my whereabouts to a person thousands of miles away, the story becomes a comedy-drama about life in a globalized world and the frustrations that can engender.

Or maybe it goes in this direction: a stranger approaches. His limp and the scar slicing across his cheek cause my hackles to rise. And here I am, all alone on this deserted stretch of road. What will happen?

In each of these instances, the inciting action is the same—the tire goes flat—but in each case, the action sends us down different narrative currents. As a writer, it's up to you to decide which current you want to paddle down. Do you want suspense? Do you prefer comedy? Or perhaps you'll choose to paddle down a current that is more about some subtle internal drama. Maybe your wife has been telling you to check the tires on this car and you've been putting it off and maybe now your story becomes all about the wear and tear in your marital relationship and how you're going to deal with that. Whichever current you choose, it will be entirely your choice. And that's what writing is all about: choices, and how to make them.

MAKING CHOICES

Sometimes, when I'm writing, I like to fancy myself a Michelangelo. I'm taking this hunk of marble and I'm bringing it to life. At points, the marble feels like an impenetrable, inert mass; at other points, I can begin to sense some form and feeling.

Other days, I'm imagining myself as a chef—Wolfgang Puck, let's say. I start out with raw ingredients—garlic, tomatoes, butter, peppers—and I'm making a sauce, cooking it down until it's so smooth and bursting with flavor that no one could possibly resist it.

The point is that whenever anyone sits down to write something—you, me, or Toni Morrison—there is the point at the beginning when you're dealing with pure matter and mass (i.e., a jumble of words) and the job of turning that into something coherent and pleasing and meaningful is a challenge. Some days I'm Wolfgang Puck, creating culinary miracles; other days, my soufflé never rises, my soup tastes like dishwater, and my chicken is worthy of a political fund-raising dinner.

Failure is always a possibility when you sit down to write something, but it helps immeasurably to have some sense of what you're actually trying to do. Just as it helps for a sculptor to have some knowledge of anatomy if he or she is going to sculpt a human form, so it will help you as a writer to have a strong grasp of the narrative form. That way, when you are faced with your inert mass, you will have some sense of what should stay and what should go.

A NARRATIVE IS . . .

What, you might ask, are you actually doing when you're writing a narrative? Easy enough. You're telling a story. In that respect, you're placing yourself squarely in a long line of storytellers—from Homer to Hugo to Dickens to Twain to Hemingway. OK, maybe you're not working on that kind of scale, but you're engaging in the very same activity that they were. They were storytellers; you're a storyteller. And a story is a story, whether it's a thousand pages long, like *Gone With the Wind*, or a one-minute joke about a rabbi, a priest, and a minister. The story can be real or it can be fictional. It can have a cast of thousands or it can all take place inside one person's head. It doesn't matter. A story is a story. A narrative is a narrative. And it has a form, even if you play with that form radically.

In this chapter, we'll be exploring the four main elements of a narrative, which I have identified as follows:

1. "The Once"
2. The Ordinary vs. The Extraordinary
3. Tension and Conflict
4. The Point

Until you understand and address those four elements, you won't really feel confident that you can tell the story as you want to tell it.

Now let's have a look at two very different storytellers to see how they spin their yarns. Imagine yourself in the office on Monday morning. There you are in the lounge, grabbing some coffee, alongside your coworkers Phil and Mike, who are also delaying the start of the workweek. What better way to procrastinate than with a story or two?

Now, Phil is a nice guy—he's always ready to help out and never has an unkind word to say about anyone—but when he starts talking, you glaze over. You just can't help it. This Monday morning, he's telling you all about how he took his dog, Ollie, to the dog park on Saturday. The one over by Monument Mountain. It's a real nice dog park. Some dog parks don't have much room for the dogs to play, but this one is real nice with trees for shade and an obstacle course and—*snore*.

Well, that's the way Phil tells a story. He never met a detail he didn't like and leaves nothing out of his narratives. Consequently, as he keeps going, you start to nod off. Even so, you get the feeling that there might be a story lurking within. Phil starts to describe this pit bull named Bonnie, and how poor Ollie was scared to death of her. But, you know, says Phil, you can't assume that just because a dog is a pit bull it means trouble. A pit bull can be a great dog.

Did you know that a hundred years ago, the pit bull was the most popular dog in America? It's people who make a dog go bad, not the dog itself. . . .

Snore, snore, and *double snore.*

As Phil continues, the story starts to develop. It seems that the dog that Ollie has been so afraid of—the fearsome Bonnie—is really a complete and utter love muffin. And that's sort of a cute story. In fact, in the hands of a real story-teller, it could be an utter charmer. But in Phil's hands, it's a monotonic soporific.

Now, Mike is a whole different story—or, should we say, he *tells* a whole different story. Mike is Irish American through and through, and proud of it. A potted shamrock grows on his windowsill and a shillelagh hangs on the wall. When Mike tells a story, he taps into centuries' worth of Irish storytelling tradition. And here, on this dreary Monday morning, he has you, along with Phil, Sandra from Accounting, and Lucas from the mail room, in thrall as he tells a story about going to his son's soccer game (we're talking about six-year-olds here) and witnessing an altercation between two moms on the opposing teams. Now there's inherent storytelling gold to be mined here—as Mike spins his yarn, you think back to Tony Soprano's loose-cannon sister Janice, punching out another mom at her kid's soccer game—but you also know that, in Phil's hands, this gold would soon be turned to dross. Mike, on the other hand, unfolds his story with impeccable timing.

The setup, the midsection, the denouement—these are all perfectly proportioned. The details are vivid and well chosen. When he describes the poodle sweatshirt of one of the moms, her whole character springs to life. In fact, chances are that if anyone should ever mention kids and soccer to you again, the first thing you'll think of is a poodle sweatshirt. That's how powerful a good image in the right place can be. And Mike doesn't drag things out. Everything is economical and to the point.

Finally, it's time to tamp down the Monday-morning resistance and get the workweek under way. But rather than remain enervated, as you were with Phil's meandering story, you're energized by the gusto of Mike's storytelling. In fact, for a quick energy charge, a story like Mike's will beat out coffee by a country mile.

"THE ONCE"

While it's fair to say that storytelling is a natural human impulse, that doesn't mean that it's easy. Some people have a natural gift for it, like Mike, which makes it easi-*er*, but, as with any activity that follows a form, be it figure skating, golf, or yoga, mistakes can and will be made. That's why it's so important to understand the form of the narrative— that is, *how the thing works.*

In order for a narrative to function as it should, it has

to address certain basic problems. As readers, we bring a set of expectations to what we read and those expectations must be met. For instance, we expect that we're not going to be bored and that when we come to the end, we're going to understand why we bothered to read this thing in the first place.

In order to meet the expectations of the reader, the writer/storyteller/narrator needs to address certain issues that apply to all narratives. The most immediate issue is how to handle time. Let's call that "The Once."

All narratives must figure out how to handle time. This issue will be especially pressing as we figure out how to have our "last say." After all, one potential goal that we've identified for these pieces is for them to be read at a funeral or memorial service. While extraordinary orators like Abraham Lincoln, Winston Churchill, and Martin Luther King Jr. could captivate audiences for an hour at a time, I think it's fair to say that most mere mortals can only hope to sustain a piece that takes no more than five minutes to deliver. A good rate of oral delivery is about 150 two-syllable words per minute, so a three- to five-minute speech (quite adequate) would be about 500 to 1,000 words.

An allotment of 500 to 1,000 words represents rather tight quarters. That means if you are writing about your trip to Machu Picchu, you can't start your story at O'Hare. There isn't enough time for you to be telling us how you checked your luggage and how you went through security and, frankly, even your closest friends and family, gathered around to hear this "last say," would not be especially interested—unless those details were somehow crucial to the point of your narrative. So you're going to have to choose just a few aspects of this life-altering trip to relate. One way you'll choose is by deciding what you can most effectively convey in the limited amount of space/time you have to work with.

"The Once" refers to that specific point in time in which the narrative is situated—like "once upon a time," the traditional opening for fairy tales. One of the most dramatic examples I can think of when it comes to managing time is Ray Bradbury's classic story "All Summer in a Day." This narrative, which is all of 983 words, is set on a distant planet where the sun appears for only one day a year. On this planet lives a victimized child named Margot, who is locked into a closet by bullies on that one day of the year when the sun comes out. "The Once" in this incredibly gripping, extremely short story is wondrously compressed, so you are right there, beside Margot, as you experience her anguish every agonizing step of the way.

Now, let's look back at the story that opened this chapter—the one that dealt with the flat tire on a typical Saturday—and let's think about how that story works in terms of managing time. Was "The Once" located in the right place? The story starts out this way:

Last Saturday, I set out to do my errands. I had the usual long list: dry cleaners, Trader Joe's, Home Depot, liquor store to pick up wine. Red, white, or rosé? We were having moussaka for dinner. I wasn't sure what went best with that, so I'd have to inquire. I stopped to get gas and picked up some Frontline at PetSmart. Then I went to the post office to buy some stamps. Then I headed home, taking the shortcut down Old Route 23, which even on a Saturday had hardly any traffic. As I headed down the road, singing along to Springsteen, I heard an ominous *thwack-thwack-thwack*. With the car rattling and shuddering, I realized I had a flat.

In just mere moments, we're going to talk a bit more about the issue of Conflict, which I've alluded to already, but it's important that you understand that your decision regarding how to handle "The Once" is going to be closely tied to the Conflict. In the above, the writer has decided to emulate the humdrum routine of a typical Saturday morning with some humdrum storytelling rhythms. That makes sense, in a certain way, but can he afford such an approach in a story of this length? Maybe not—and perhaps some of those humdrum details could be pruned back. Let's look at this story in a version that handles "The Once" in a very different way:

As I headed down Old Route 23, I had the road to myself. After a Saturday morning filled with chores and errands, I was letting off some steam, singing along to Springsteen as I cruised along. Suddenly, I heard an ominous *thwack-thwack-thwack*. With the car rattling and shuddering, I realized I had a flat.

As you can see, this approach handles time in a much more compressed way, but maybe it doesn't take *enough* time now. Maybe it feels rushed and unbaked. This is the kind of thing that you have to develop a feeling for—where, precisely, to pick up your story.

You might even play around with going in a more radical direction by locating "The Once" this way:

Thwack-thwack-thwack.
That ominous sound brought everything to a sharp halt: my Saturday morning, comfortably filled with errands, and my drive down Old Route 23, which I had all to myself.
Thwack-thwack-thwack.
Damn it. I had a flat tire. So what now?

As you can see, this version handles the issue of "The Once" by relying on the tried-and-true literary convention of *in medias res*—starting in the "middle of things."

We'll say more about that later, but the point is that an opening like that can buy you time and can grab a reader's attention.

THE ORDINARY VS.
THE EXTRAORDINARY

The second basic problem that writers have to address when constructing a narrative is to figure out the "Extraordinary" thing that is going to ignite it. A story deserves to be told only when there is something out of the ordinary within it. The story of my Saturday morning peregrinations does not deserve to be told if it only covers my stops at the dry cleaners, Trader Joe's, and the liquor store. But when I get a flat tire, the *Extraordinary* thing occurs—that is, the thing that is *out of the ordinary*—and so the story begins to unfold.

Similarly, in the case of poor, dull Phil, the account of taking his dog, Ollie, to the dog park is not a story; it's simply an incident. And, in that sense, it has no more weight or narrative drive than any number of incidents that Phil might have been involved with on his weekend: shopping, planting tomatoes, eating brunch. The thing that gets the story going is when Ollie spots Bonnie, the pit bull, who he fears. In other words, Conflict rears its head. And then

The Ordinary vs. The Extraordinary comes into play when the pit bull turns out to be a sweetheart—and Ollie's expectations, as well as ours, undergo a 360° turn.

As for Mike's story, it artfully showcases the contrast between The Ordinary and The Extraordinary. He starts out with a very *Ordinary* situation—a kids' soccer game—and suddenly something *Extraordinary* emerges in the form of a brawl between two moms. Who could resist finding out more about that one?

TENSION AND CONFLICT

Whether we receive a narrative orally or by reading it, one of the things we will surely want to find out is how that *Extraordinary* event is ultimately going to help resolve the Tension and Conflict that act as another kind of frame for the piece.

Now it's important that you understand that any narrative is bound to have several frames that interact with one another—and with the audience. One frame, which we've been discussing, is the time sequence of the narrative—whether it's a picnic, a raft ride, an intimate conversation, a gymnastics performance, a walk with the dog, or a hundred other "pieces of time." Superimposed onto that frame is the Tension and Conflict frame. When I get a flat tire on a busy Saturday morning, that occurrence takes place in the context of something bigger. Was I feeling harried and discontented? Did I have a fight with my wife before I left? Is it my birthday tomorrow and I'm freaking out about turning 65? Is this the first time in a very long time that I am feeling that things are actually pretty good—I've gotten over my health scare and work is plentiful—and then, wham, the tire goes flat and I'm pitched back into a down mood?

Now let's look back at Mike's story of the brawl between the soccer moms. Here the narrative would gain richness if this odd event were set in a context that reflected some of the Tension and Conflict that Mike was experiencing. Nothing in life is neutral, you know, so what could Mike have been feeling when he was sitting at his son's game on that Saturday morning? Did he feel happy to be there and thus outraged when the rude interruption of the soccer moms came along? A simple story, but potentially an effective one. Or did he feel that he was sick of soccer, sick of crazy parents, and wanted no more part of any of this? A somewhat more complex story, with more Tension and Conflict. Or did he feel that he, too, on more than one occasion, had been a crazy soccer parent and that this bizarre incident was a reality check that saved him from repeating another such embarrassing situation? A more complex story, with more interesting Tension and Conflict. In other words, a better story.

THE POINT

By the time you've reached the end of the narrative—whether you're writing it or reading it—you should have the answer to the question, *Why?* This is the question that lies at the heart of all narratives. Why am I reading this? Why did I bother? What did I get out of it? What's *The Point* of it all?

Sometimes The Point of a narrative is made absolutely explicit, as in Aesop's fables. Whether the fables are about milkmaids, foxes, or hares, The Point (or moral) is clearly stated at the end. A desperately thirsty crow finds a pitcher but cannot reach the water because the level is too low and his beak cannot reach it. After trying many different approaches, the crow drops stones into the pitcher until the level of the water rises to meet his beak. The Point of the story? *Necessity is the mother of invention.*

While there is certainly pleasure to be had in reading a story whose point is so simply and explicitly stated, there is perhaps more pleasure to be had, particularly for the more mature reader, when The Point doesn't jump out at you and shake you by the hand. The Point of a narrative can be subtle, even elusive. Some of the best narratives require that you spend time thinking about what it is that you've just read and what, in fact, The Point might be.

What is The Point in the flat-tire story? Well, that all

depends on which current you have chosen to sail down. If it's the one about mounting complications (missing jack, limp spare, dead phone), The Point could be as simple as *Be prepared.* (This is, in fact, so simple a point that you might consider going back and rethinking the current you've chosen, aiming this time for something a bit more complex.) In the current that sends you into the interaction with the Indian person at a call center thousands of miles away, the story might turn out to be one in which your preconceptions are blown out of the water when you discover that the Indian person is far more effective and compassionate than you could possibly have imagined. Here, The Point might be something like, *Avoid stereotypes and keep an open mind.* Now let's imagine we've gone down the current that features that ominous-looking "Good Samaritan." If this person is really dangerous, and I manage to get away, then The Point might be, *Always keep your head in a crisis.* If the ominous-looking man turns out to be a good and helpful person, then The Point might be, *Don't judge a book by its cover.* (These "points" are stated as clichés, as you can see, but just keep in mind that we're only using shorthand here to capture the spirit of The Point. I certainly wouldn't encourage anyone to state such points explicitly.)

Ultimately, we may decide that none of these points is interesting enough to justify the telling of these stories, but at least there is a kernel of potential within each of them.

CONFLICT IS . . .

I've been using the term *Conflict* all along, but now I'd like to expand on that subject a bit. Simply put, Conflict is the struggle between opposing forces—for our purposes, between you, the protagonist, and whatever is coming up against you. Conflicts can exist between individual characters (think of Stephen King's *Misery*, with Paul Sheldon, trapped with broken legs, pitted against Annie Wilkes, the psychotic former nurse). Conflicts can be between groups of characters (how about the Lannisters and the Starks in *Game of Thrones?*), between individuals and society (the bank officer Joseph K. and The State in Franz Kafka's *The Trial*), between individuals and the physical world (James Franco, trapped in a cave, in *127 Hours*), or between individuals and their own demons (*Dr. Jekyll and Mr. Hyde*). The Conflict can be supremely easy to identify and figure out, as in fairy tales—Hansel and Gretel vs. the Witch, the Three Little Pigs vs. the Wolf—or it can be quite complicated, often with a central character who is not even aware of his or her Conflict until it's too late (Jay Gatsby in *The Great Gatsby*).

Classical storytelling is characterized by certain consistent elements. Among these are protagonists who are active, who deal with external Conflict in continuous time and reality, and who, at the end, find a neatly wrapped (though sometimes tragic) resolution. Hercules, Pocahontas, and Robin Hood are all examples of classical heroes.

Modern heroes operate differently. Here the emphasis is often on internal Conflict, sometimes with a passive protagonist who exists within an anti-structure where time and reality are not continuous or consistent and where things are not neatly wrapped up at the end. Yossarian in Joseph Heller's *Catch-22*, Lisbeth Salander in *The Girl with the Dragon Tattoo*, and Holden Caulfield in J. D. Salinger's *The Catcher in the Rye* are good examples of the modern hero.

In the writing challenge that you're taking on—"the last say"—I guess it's conceivable to portray yourself as a classical hero. Maybe you're going to be telling the story of how you rode out a hurricane strapped to the mast of a boat or faced down a mob intent on doing an injustice. I would wager, however, that most of you will go in the other direction, portraying yourself as a modern hero with warts and all. At least, every person I have ever worked with around this assignment has gone in that direction. After all, this is a form of life review and most of us, in this complicated world that we live in, see ourselves as complicated players in that world, possessed of strengths and plagued by weaknesses, enjoying triumphs and surviving setbacks.

MAKING A STORY

In our next chapter, we will return to the issue of Conflict when we discuss topics to write about. For now, however, I'd like to show you what I came up with for an essay that uses the flat tire as a springboard. See whether you think I've created a narrative that solves all the problems we've been exploring in this chapter.

I was always a person who sweated the small stuff. That's just the way I was raised. My parents regarded the loss of an umbrella as a tragic event and so, throughout my life, I have tended to see disaster lurking around every corner. But one day, a few years ago, in the course of my usual Saturday morning routine of running errands, something changed for me.

It was almost noon and I had completed my whole list of assignments. I bought the mirror hangers and the grout cleaner at Home Depot. I got the avocados, the soy chips, and the Greek yogurt at Trader Joe's. I picked up the dry cleaning. I bought the wine for dinner. As I was heading home on Old Route 23, I had Bruce Springsteen amped up on the CD player and was singing along to "Badlands" when all of a sudden I heard something.

Thwack-thwack-thwack.

For a moment I wanted to believe that I had driven over something, like a cardboard box, but then the thwacking got louder, the car got wobblier, and I knew I had a flat.

From that point forward, the misadventures began to pile up. My jack was missing and I could see that, even if I had one, the spare was low on air. To compound these problems, my cell was out of its charge. Natalie had cautioned me to recharge my phone, but I had a tendency to be lax in that regard and so here I was, paying the price.

Sitting on the side of the road, which had become deserted in the years since they built the bypass, I wondered how I was going to get out of there. I mean, I was really stuck. I started to think about what a screwup I was. How was I going to explain to people, including my wife, that I was so ill prepared? And then, as I ran through my repertoire of self-recrimination, I realized that I was listening to old voices telling me old things and I didn't want to hear them. I wanted to think along entirely different lines, burning altogether new brain pathways, and, with a deep breath, I told myself that somehow it would all work itself out.

It was a beautiful day. The sun was out and there was a cool, refreshing breeze. I propped up the hood of the car—the universal distress signal—and sat reading my book, William Faulkner's *Light in August*, for maybe an hour. I refused to feel stress or shame. Finally, another vehicle appeared on the road. A guy in a truck, actually, who had just what I needed to get going. I tried to pay him something, but he wouldn't take it, which only added another layer of enlightenment to my day.

What a fine morning it had been, I thought, as I pulled out onto Old Route 23, singing along to Springsteen, louder than ever. I realized that I had made a breakthrough that day. I learned to treat myself kindly and I learned to be open to the kindness of others.

So here I've taken the setup that we've been talking about—a flat tire on a busy Saturday morning—and I've used it as a prompt to write a story in about 520 words. Let's see if it has addressed the issues of the narrative that I've laid out.

Regarding "The Once," it establishes its moment of time in the first paragraph: the usual Saturday morning routine of running errands. Check.

With regard to The Ordinary vs. The Extraordinary, the Extraordinary kicks in when the tire goes flat (*thwack-thwack-thwack*). The tedium of the errand-laden Saturday morning gives way to something quite different in nature. Check.

As for Tension and Conflict, that's interesting to consider. The fragment with which we started this chapter described the flat tire but offered no Tension and Conflict beyond the actual incident. In this "evolved" story, the Tension and Conflict are psychological in nature. Here is a person who has always sweated the small stuff, and when the Extraordinary thing happens—the flat on a deserted road—he is brought nose to nose with his problematic worldview. Check.

Finally, we have The Point. It is laid out quite explicitly. Treat yourself kindly and be open to the kindness of others. In its small way, this incident has become something of a game changer for this writer . . . and something that he wants the people in his life to know about. Check.

Is this a brilliant work of art? Hardly. Could it be better? Yes . . . always. And as you write your "last say" (and as you'll see with my "last say" coming right up), what we are striving for with our pieces will far outstrip what you have just read. But keep in mind, too, that this essay, which I wrote as a mere exercise to prove some points I was making, took me perhaps all of ten minutes to write. Then again, I'm a professional writer who is not fazed by the prospect of making choices, so a story like this, created as a simple teaching tool, goes quickly for me.

You, however, are most likely *not* a professional writer—but that certainly doesn't mean you can't powerfully capture your "last say." The point of this book is to allow anyone and everyone to understand how a narrative works and how to write one. As we move along in the book, we'll be examining all the choices we have to make—point of view, style, tone—but, right now, in the chapter coming up next, we'll look at how you can locate a topic to write about.

The Last Say: Alan

OK, people. By now, I am imagining that at least some of you are scratching your heads. "What the heck does one of these 'last says' actually look like?" you're wondering. That's a reasonable question and, to answer it, I'd like to offer up the first of the "last says" that you'll be encountering in this book. This one is by yours truly.

When I envisioned this project and imagined myself explaining to people what this was all about, I realized that I had better write a "last say" myself, to use as a model. So I started thinking about my whole long complicated life and which incidents might lend themselves to being turned into the kind of narratives that would pass along a value, impart some kind of life lesson, or otherwise show something about myself that I would want others to know and remember.

It didn't take long for me to retrieve from my memory bank an incident that took place more than fifteen years ago. It was something I had always wanted to write about, but life got in the way. Even so, this memory had stuck in my mind, assuming an importance I didn't fully understand—until I wrote about it. As soon as I wrote this

piece, it became clear why the incident had been so important to me.

So, without further ado, let me present my "last say."
Please understand, however, that this is just a label I'm putting on this piece for now—a kind of placeholder, if you
will. As a writer, I reserve the right to have other "last says"
before I'm done. As, of course, you will, too. We are all entitled to multiple "last says," for we all have many stories to
share and our values and perspectives can certainly change.

There I stood, on the Main Concourse of Grand Central Terminal, at the information booth, as planned,
holding a bag of hot pretzels from Zaro's, looking
around in every direction. It was Friday afternoon of a
long summer weekend and everyone seemed to have
somewhere to get to. It occurred to me that Noah might
be late, but then I saw him, my son, coming toward me
in the surge of people. Nineteen years old, baseball cap,
tattered jeans, flip-flops, duffel bag, smile, wave, and
off we went to board our train, finding seats that faced
the right way, and settling in for the two-hour trip to
Wassaic, where we would pick up our car and drive the
extra hour home.

Following the pretzels and a few perfunctory replies
to my questions about his summer internship, Noah fell
asleep. In that July heat, the drool collected at the corner of his shiny lip, just as it used to in his stroller. I

kicked off my shoes and looked around at all the men in their summer gabardine suits, jackets folded and stashed away, ties loosened, laptops out. I closed my eyes, too, and then, in that damp half state between sleep and waking, my mind wandered to memories of my own father, a man in a gray flannel suit, who every now and then would take me to the city with him on the commuter train from Scarsdale. In such moments of rare, uncomfortable proximity, my father would attempt to instruct me in worldly skills, like the proper way to fold the *New York Times*. For my father, who based his life on mastering rituals, this action was as prescribed and formal as the folding of a military flag. I watched and ignored in equal measure. What had I taught my sons? I wondered, as I drifted through the half-sleep.

Then there was a startling whistle and a few minutes before the train was due to arrive in Wassaic, Noah and I gathered our things and stood in the aisle. Behind me, a man approximately my age was craning to look out the window and seemed agitated. He asked me which station this was and when I told him, he said that he had slept right through Dover Plains, the station before, and didn't know how he was going to get back to his car. As Dover Plains was only a few minutes' detour, I offered to drive him. Along the way, we chatted. He told us he was a professor of art at Yale; I told him I was a writer. When we dropped him off at his car, he thanked me profusely and said to Noah, "Your father is a gentleman."

Back on the road, heading north on 22, Noah and I drove in silence for a few miles. Finally, he spoke.

"Why did you do that?" he asked, with an edge of annoyance in his voice.

I knew where the edge was coming from. He was challenging me to tell a truth and was wary that I might not produce one.

"You must always, always do the good thing," I said.

And that was enough. With a sideways glance, I saw him thinking about it. Then he put on a CD and for the rest of the trip home we listened to Dylan.

When I wrote this and then sat back to consider my creation, it came as no surprise to me that I had used the opportunity of this "last say" to explore my role as a father. Of the various roles I've assumed in the course of my life-time, being a father is certainly my Hamlet/King Lear/Othello rolled into one. It is a role I initially assumed with trepidation, but, over time, I came to realize that I had something of a calling for it. When I think back on my life and imagine people gathered around to remember me, I feel that the principal way I would want to be remembered is as a father.

Of course, any father or mother can tell you that the

condition of being a parent involves a vast array of experiences, so why did I happen to zero in on this one? To answer that question, let's examine this narrative to see if I met and resolved the issues that I faced when I started out on this assignment.

Did I deal with "The Once" successfully? I think so. This story is set on a "Friday afternoon of a long summer weekend." It's also set at a point in time when my son was nineteen years old. He's considerably older than that now, so those who know me—that is, those who would be interested enough to gather around to hear my "last say"—would recognize that this is a reflective piece. Those who don't know me personally might also deduce that this is a reflective piece from the tone, but we'll talk more about tone as we move ahead in the book. So, yes—I've situated this story in time, and I've picked it up at the point where I'm waiting for my son to meet me in the train station, just before he actually appears. The reason for that choice? Because I wanted the reader/listener to witness the effect that seeing my son had on me as he came into view.

The next issue on the list is The Ordinary vs. The Extraordinary. It's interesting the way this story addresses that issue. Nothing Extraordinary happens here until the other passenger fails to get off at his station. Before that, everything in this story deals with The Ordinary. So was that a big mistake to wait until more than halfway through the story to get to the Extraordinary thing? You tell me, but, as far as I'm concerned, who ever said that the Extraordinary thing has to come at the top of the story? If you place it further along, as I have, that placement can turn out to be quite effective. The only caveat is that you have to be able to sustain a sense of momentum until you get to the Extraordinary thing, and that can be challenging for the less experienced writer. (Situating your story on a train, with its propulsive forward movement, is a good way to ward off a sense of stasis.)

Now we come to Tension and Conflict. Lord knows I've had plenty of that in my life (what writer hasn't?), so I wasn't too worried about locating that subtext. As I see it, the Tension and Conflict in this story is most apparent in the second paragraph—particularly in the phrase, *What had I taught my sons?* Right before that, I had evoked a memory of traveling on a train with my own father, with whom I had a somewhat conflicted relationship, and this paragraph alludes very subtly to those strains. That memory brings me to the crucial question—*What had I taught my sons?*—and lays the groundwork for The Point.

Ah, The Point. Can't leave home without one. The Point in my story is stated quite explicitly—almost like a moral. *You must always, always do the good thing.* In fact, I don't think I was an especially directive father—much more of a laid-back one (but you'd have to ask my sons)—except I remember how that moment jumped out at me as such a teaching moment. Perhaps that is why this story popped into my head and begged to be told when I was fishing around for my "last say"—because it was so atypical and because it contained a value that I felt strongly about, that I feel I have lived by, and that I wanted to pass on.

So what do you think? Did I succeed?

CHAPTER 2

Finding Your Topic

When I first began to approach people with the idea of working on this assignment, I found myself getting a series of unmistakable deer-in-the-headlights reactions. To these folks, the prospect of looking back over their lives and picking out one story that would somehow serve as their legacy was overwhelming. And, now that I think about it, why wouldn't it be? After all, our lives are packed with stories and incidents and events. How can we pick out just one—and how can we tell it effectively? The good news is that I have devised a method by which the average person can look back over his or her life in a systematic and expeditious way and thereby find a topic that will lend itself to a "last say."

THE BLANK PAGE

What should I write about?

That question haunts all writers as they sit down in front of a computer screen, a notebook, a napkin, or wherever else they might think to express themselves. Many of you have already experienced the genuine agony that comes with confronting a tabula rasa at the beginning of the writing process. Douglas Adams, author of the classic comic novel *The Hitchhiker's Guide to the Galaxy*, captured that agony perfectly when he said, "Writing is easy. You only need to stare at a piece of paper until your forehead bleeds." Take heart, however, and know that the "staring" part of the writing process cannot be sidestepped. It simply comes with the territory.

I've been a professional writer all of my adult life, and I still "stare" whenever I sit down to write. I'll suddenly find something in my office that urgently needs cleaning—like the walls—and will distract myself for as long as it takes until my self-discipline reasserts itself. If you are committed to the task, you will get beyond this phase. Just allow time for your self-discipline to kick in and understand that if you're staring or doodling or whatever, you're doing the hardest part of the work: confronting and overcoming the fear.

Procrastination, which can emerge in response to this

kind of fear, is perhaps most easily dealt with through the application of an external motivator. My high school students who are writing their college admissions essays have a powerful external motivator. They know that if they don't get their essays done by the time the admissions packet has to be submitted, they will not be playing beer pong beyond the jurisdiction of their parents come fall. I have a good external motivator, as I make my living as a writer. I know that if I don't write, my income will grind to a halt and my bills will go unpaid. These external motivators do not altogether trump the fear of failure, but they do help get you over the hump. I suspect, however, that the question many of you are asking yourselves right now is why you should bother taking on this assignment altogether. After all, no one is forcing you to have your "last say." Might you not be better off going out to brunch? Admittedly, it's a lot easier to sit at a sidewalk café on a beautiful day eating eggs Benedict than it is to stare at a blank slate. So why pursue this project at all?

WHY, INDEED?

There are many reasons why people write—to connect, to come to terms with something in the past, to project into the future, to amuse, to arouse, to confess, to forgive—but one of the best reasons, although it is not stated as such, comes from that excellent teacher, Natalie Goldberg, author of *Writing Down the Bones.* "Writers live twice," said Goldberg.

I think that all great writers engage in an unspoken quest for immortality when they set out to write something, and I think that, to some extent, this quest strikes at the heart of what we're trying to do here as well. We are thinking that if our "last says" are good enough, they may be passed down from generation to generation, allowing a little piece of us to live on. And do you know what? If they're good enough, that might actually happen. But, even if they don't help you achieve immortality, they can go a long way toward helping you gain perspective on the life you've lived.

To my way of thinking, this kind of life review is nothing but positive. When you write an essay such as the ones you will be reading in this book, you are engaged in work that is really not that different from the work that Faulkner and Dostoyevsky and Virginia Woolf were engaged in. Just as they were looking to bring meaning to the human experience, so, too, are you looking to bring meaning to *your* human experience. Of course, they were working on an entirely different scale with a radically different set of skills, but there is definitely an analogy to be drawn. And this is why, when I find myself working with nonprofessional writers who are crafting their "last says," I often feel the same sense of excitement and exhilaration that I feel whenever I read good writing. I admire the commitment. I admire the courage. And I admire the ability of people—"ordinary" people, if you will—to reflect on their lives, find meaning in their experiences, and, through rigorous application of craft, shape their writing so that others can understand and appreciate what they have set out to express.

RELEVANCY AND RESISTANCE

With this particular assignment, there may be yet another problematic plateau to get beyond, so, before we go any further, I'd like to address that. Let me begin by telling you a very short story.

The other day I was in a synagogue board meeting and one of my fellow trustees said something that stuck in my mind. This fellow, who I'll call Matt, is the opposite of a shrinking violet (an in-your-face violet?). He has an opinion, often a good one, on almost everything and, while he knows how to wait his turn to talk, he takes many turns. He has been a faculty member at a major university for over 30 years, which means that he has essentially been living in meetings, and what he said stunned me. "Now when I go into a meeting, no one hears me," claimed Matt, who is 62.

I suspect that what Matt was saying was untrue—I can't imagine him *not* being heard—but certainly the feeling he was expressing was an authentic one that many of us have experienced. Not being heard and not being seen is one of the occupational hazards of being an older person. I have often heard older women bemoan the fact that when they walk down the street, people don't turn around to look at them anymore. Many of us have had the experience of going into a restaurant that primarily caters to a young crowd and we have found ourselves almost completely ignored by the staff. And, of course, those who are retired may be feeling issues around relevancy even more acutely. Are we earning the air we breathe if we are not involved in real work?

When I'm not writing about writing, I am usually writing development and recruitment materials for colleges and universities. This is something I've been doing for years, and I've worked with blue-chip clients like Vanderbilt University, Rensselaer Polytechnic Institute, Hunter College, Union College, and the Culinary Institute of America. My job usually involves going to a college campus at the beginning of the assignment to meet with the cast of characters, which usually includes a director of enrollment management, a director of publications, assistant directors thereof, faculty members, and so on.

I have begun to notice that when I'm in such a meeting now, I am often the oldest person in the room—often by ten or even 20 years. And that means that when I walk into that room, people look at me and wonder what I'm doing there. And, in all modesty, let me say that I look *fabulous* for

63—but who am I kidding? Sixty-three does not look like 43, which does not look like 23.

And then, in this room full of young or youngish strangers, I have to overcome the stigma. And I do that by using my mind, solving problems, sharing expertise, and doing all the things that I have always been very good at . . . *and that I am still very good at.* And then the age barriers fall away, more or less, and we are collaborators, agreeing, disagreeing, engaged with one another.

The Point of this story is that the best remedy I know of for irrelevancy—or, otherwise put, the best way to stay *relevant*—is to use your mind. When you can contribute sharp thinking, informed opinions, judgment that is rooted in experience, then you will never be irrelevant, no matter how old you are.

I'm drawing particular attention to this issue right now because I have noticed that one of the inhibiting factors I see among people who take on this assignment is that they are afraid that they might not be able to produce work that others will be interested in. They are infected with that oppressive feeling of irrelevancy that can afflict people of a certain age—and so they are resistant to sitting down and doing the work. To these folks, I say, *The work is the cure.* Engaging in this kind of life review with the discipline that is required when you write for an audience is nothing less than revivifying.

SELF-EXAMINATION

I think it's fair to say that curiosity is a fundamental part of a writer's job description. Take my own story, for instance. At a certain point in my career, after having published fiction and nothing else, something happened to send my life in an entirely new direction. My wife and I owned a vacation home in a rural area of upstate New York, and a boy who lived just a few doors down from us killed four members of his family. I was plunged into this tragic event when the police came to my door in the middle of that awful night to ask if I had seen anything unusual. Although I had no background as a journalist and was naturally daunted by the idea of writing about an event that was so real and so complicated, I was also curious. Indeed, I told myself that if I were not curious about a murder that had occurred virtually in my backyard, then perhaps I should pursue some other vocational direction. Raising alpacas, perhaps?

No, no. I was and had always been a writer, and so I rose to the occasion, simply by starting to ask questions. And that is precisely what you're going to be doing. You're going to ask yourself questions and you're going to answer them in a way that is fast and almost reflexive. The idea is to insert a metaphorical dipstick into your brain to see what's going on in there.

Here are some questions to start with:

- What has been the hardest thing in my life?
- If I had to quickly replay my life, which two or three moments would jump out ahead of all the others?
- Who is the person who has surprised me the most?
- When have my mind and body felt in perfect harmony?
- Which experiences have really pulled me out of my comfort zone?
- Have I ever changed the course of someone else's life?
- Do I believe in a higher being? If so, how?
- What is my idea of a perfect day?
- Which personal weaknesses have I worked on the hardest?
- What have I done that "they" said couldn't be done?
- What fills me with pride?
- When did my mind and body feel utterly out of sync?
- Which of my relationships have I worked at the hardest?
- Have I ever made a discovery that thrilled me?
- What do I regard as my greatest victory?
- What in the world utterly fascinates me?

- At which points have I felt inadequate and how did I deal with those feelings?
- What object or possession holds the most meaning for me?
- If I can't sleep at night, what's keeping me up?
- When I close my eyes and picture a place in the world that is special to me, which place is that?
- Have I ever experienced a genuine life-changer?
- Have I ever felt betrayed?
- How have I changed over the course of my lifetime?
- What would I choose to be remembered for?
- Why do I consider life to be worth living?
- Is there a work of art that truly reflects my worldview?
- What will I miss most when I'm gone?
- Which of life's mysteries have I unraveled?
- What was my most embarrassing moment?
- Have I ever freed myself of a compulsion?
- Which of life's complications am I still struggling with?
- What makes me laugh?
- Where am I most at home and why?

Whew. Now, that was a whirlwind tour of your psyche, wasn't it? Are you feeling a little overwhelmed perhaps?

Maybe even shaking your head, convinced that I'm leading you into the Valley of Clichés?

My most embarrassing moment? Are you kidding me?

Actually, I'm completely serious—and absolutely dedicated to making sure that you avoid all that is trite, commonplace, or shallow. The goal in asking these questions is simply to point you in a direction. After all, you have a lot of living under your belt, so the idea of singling out a moment or two can certainly feel overwhelming at first. But don't worry—you're not alone. Your mind is there to help you. Answer each question quickly, in just a sentence or two, and then, over the course of four or five days, return to your answers and note which ones you are being pulled back to. If it's the Most Embarrassing, know that you're being led there for a reason. If there's something that's keeping you up at night (i.e., your answer to the question, "If I can't sleep at night, what's keeping me up?"), then pay attention because this is a subject that may warrant further exploration. If the word *betrayed* is flashing on and off in your mind like a neon sign (in response to the question "Have I ever felt betrayed?"), give it room.

You'll also want to explore whether there are any connections to be drawn among your responses. In the next sample essay, which is coming right up, you'll see how connections can be made and how these connections can help you achieve a resonance that might not otherwise be achieved if you were simply to tackle a topic point-on.

As you weigh your answers to these questions, just remember that the rules of writing a narrative remain the same no matter which writing topic you ultimately choose. First of all, you're going to have to figure out "The Once"—that is, when to pick up the narrative and when to leave it off.

From there, you'll go on to The Ordinary vs. The Extraordinary. Is something actually happening in your story? There had better be. And that issue is closely related to the matter of Conflict and Tension. As we have said, Conflict is the engine that drives all great writing, and it will be driving your writing, too. Sometimes that Conflict is very obvious. When we read Stephen King's *Cujo*, we can see, right away, that the Conflict comes in the form of a massive, mouth-foaming, rabid Saint Bernard and the Tension is about whether that mother and her son can get out of their sweltering, suffocating car and past the behemoth. Sometimes the Conflict is subtle, and it can take a while to figure out what's going on, as is the case of something like Virginia Woolf's *Mrs. Dalloway*. What actually is the Conflict for this middle-aged woman going about her errands, preparing to host a party? You, the reader, have to figure that out.

Please understand as well that comedy is also all about Conflict—whether it's getting a banana cream pie in the face, as in old-time burlesque routines, or whether it's Woody Allen meeting Diane Keaton's family in *Annie Hall*. Conflict need not be focused only on issues of illness, loss, and so on.

The Conflict that you choose to write about, whether it's obvious, subtle, comic, internal, or external, is likely to be something that has been on your mind and in your heart for many years. As you approach this assignment, answering these exploratory questions and settling on a topic, you may be genuinely surprised by the topic you ultimately land on. Not to worry, though. Surprise can be good—both for the reader/listener and for the writer.

The Last Say: **Anne**

For me, working with a person on his or her "last say" has been fascinating— particularly when I have known that person for many years. Such was the case with Anne, a good friend for more than two decades. Anne knew that I was looking for "subjects" to help me develop my theories around this work, and she gallantly submitted to the exercise. I was so glad to have her aboard, as I knew she was a highly sensitive person with a love of language and an interesting, complicated life upon which to draw.

As always, the process began with the exploratory questions presented in this chapter. Anne's answers, like Anne herself, were honest, rich, and distinctive. To the question, "What has been the hardest thing in my life?" Anne's responses included "giving up cigarettes—trying, failing, trying—dealing with shame." To the question, "When have my mind and body felt in perfect harmony?"

she cited singing in choir. And to the question, "Which experiences have really pulled me out of my comfort zone?" one of her answers included, "Singing in public, in front of people who expect you to be good."

After going back and forth for a while on the issue of the topic, Anne made her call. In an e-mail to me, she wrote, "I think I will write about singing, but from a slightly different angle—all about learning to breathe, how and when to do it, and the power it gives you. And how breathing in concert with a close group of people helps you breathe on your own." I thought that sounded like it had potential, and Anne did a great first draft.

As much as I admired her first draft, however, I still felt that something was missing. To me, the best essays have layers of meaning. So far, Anne's wasn't digging down quite deep enough. Then I thought of the fact that she had been dealing with chronic obstructive pulmonary disease (COPD), and it all came together. The smoking, the COPD, the shame, the singing—and ultimately the life affirmation. That quality-of-life affirmation is really what Anne is about and it's the value that she chose to convey to friends and family in her "last say."

Here is her essay:

I shape my lips into a round, "aw"-shaped smile and inhale deeply. All around me I hear the sound of circular breathing, feeling its warm and sustaining force.

Justina, our director, nods, and we exhale the first chord of Cristobal de Morales's "Alleluia." It's true, in sync, in tune. We're really together this afternoon.

It's deep winter, and the audience that fills this small drafty New England church is swathed in sweaters and scarves. We nine singers are also wearing close-fitting hats in solidarity with Laurel, our soprano soloist, a recent cancer survivor. We're all in various stages of middle age, busy with our lives, but not even a blizzard could keep us away from this recital.

Suddenly I can feel my chest tightening. It's almost time for the last song. I'll be starting the solo, and there won't be a music folder or a microphone to grab on to for support. "No props, just you," as Justina likes to say.

This squeezing out of air has happened before. The first time I stood in front of this group to sing about eight bars of a folk song, I felt suddenly stunned, like a cow in the slaughter line. I couldn't remember how to breathe. The first note came out as a croak, and the phrase wavered along from there. The next phrase was a little better, but there was no strength or conviction behind it. My cheeks were burning as I stepped back into the group.

That was five years ago, and the shortness of breath was mostly due to anxiety. Now emphysema has been added to the challenge, and sometimes it feels as though

I'm inhaling through mesh. It's my own fault, of course. If I allow myself to think about it, my thirty-five years of smoking point accusing fingers at me; then my throat goes dry, which makes it even harder to sing. I actually stayed away from singing for many years, as much as I loved it, because I was afraid to try and fail. An extremely wise musical friend finally steered me to Justina, who convinced me I could do it and that it would actually feel good.

As the cycles of my breath have gotten shorter, I've spoken to Justina about my concern that I'll become a liability to the group. Should I give it up? But Justina has said no. If I keep working on my breathing, singing will be the best thing for me; and even if I'm not consciously aware of it, she and the others will be helping.

I step in front of the group with Laurel, my friend and duet partner. The piano gives us our notes and the chorus begins humming, four chords up, four chords down, then one more time. In spite of Laurel's reassuring presence and the warmth I can feel behind me, my chest starts tightening up. This time I know what to do.

My feet feel for the solid floor, my shoulders relax. I don't know how many more recitals I have ahead of me, but right now that doesn't matter. Four beats before my first note the inhale begins, through "aw"-shaped mouth, expanding abdomen and chest, flowing down the legs, connecting with the live earth. Then the breath *wants* to come back out, toward the tip of the nose, over the heads in front of me, toward the high stained glass window on the back wall. My voice wants to come with it, and does.

Lean on me, when you're not strong,

It's all about the breath. I can feel all nine of us taking a common inhale. Laurel and I smile at each other, and everyone sings the chorus:

and I'll be your friend. I'll help you carry on.

Then Laurel begins the next verse an octave above, so clear and full of feeling. It's working, for both of us, for today at least. We're breathing, and singing.

Aaaahhhh.

Do you admire the candor and craft of this essay as much as I do? I kind of bet you do. After all, it addresses all the "must-haves" of a narrative—and then, once those elements are in place, it takes it to the next level of emotional connection, reflection, and renewal.

Splendid job, Anne.

CHAPTER 3

Point of View

Chances are, it's been a while since you've had an English class and so you may have forgotten all those things you learned way back when, like iambic pentameter, onomatopoeia, synecdoche, and so forth. To tell you the truth, I've forgotten some of them as well. Some things are more important than others, however, and if you're going to write a narrative, it is imperative that you have some understanding of what point of view is all about.

Point of view, succinctly defined, means the vantage point from which a writer passes the narrative on to the reader. There are three factors that determine point of view: person, number, and tense.

PERSON

With regard to the *person* point of view, your options are not exactly dizzying. There are exactly three: first person, second person, and third person.

First Person

Think back to some of the books that made you fall in love with reading and let's look at the language that captivated you:

- You don't know about me without you have read a book by the name of *The Adventures of Tom Sawyer*; but that ain't no matter. That book was made by Mr. Mark Twain, and he told the truth, mainly. There was things which he stretched, but mainly he told the truth.

- I, Tiberius Claudius Drusus Nero Germanicus This-that-and-the-other (for I shall not trouble you yet with all my titles) who was once, and not long ago either, known to my friends and relatives and associates as "Claudius the Idiot," or "Clau-Clau-Claudius" or at best as "Poor Uncle Claudius,"

am now about to write this strange history of my
life . . .

- Lolita, light of my fire, fire of my loins. My sin,
  my soul. Lo-lee-ta: the tip of the tongue taking a
  trip of three steps down the palate to tap, at three,
  on the teeth. Lo. Lee. Ta.

There you have the voices of Mark Twain's Huckle-
berry Finn, the Roman emperor Claudius in Robert
Graves's *I, Claudius,* and Humbert Humbert in Vladimir
Nabokov's *Lolita.* In most cases, whenever a reader encoun-
ters a first-person voice such as those above, that reader
tends to feel more connected to the story. And that doesn't
only happen when that first-person voice is coming from a
main character. Connectedness is also cultivated when the
first-person voice belongs to a supporting character who
is telling the story, as with Nick Carraway in *The Great
Gatsby,* the Chief in *One Flew Over the Cuckoo's Nest,* or
Nelly Dean in *Wuthering Heights.*

Now it's very likely that your "last say" will be told in
your first-person voice. In fact, it might be virtually impossible for you to imagine telling the story any other way.
That's fine, and probably as it should be, but keep in mind
that the best writing is often about breaking rules. So while
first person could certainly be the right direction for your
piece, at least be aware of your other options . . . of which
there are exactly two.

Second Person

As a reader of a certain age, you may have come this far in your life without ever having read any fiction told in the second person. A second-person point of view is not one that you will normally (or perhaps ever) encounter. There are, however, certain instances where it is used effectively in literature. Check out Tom Robbins's *Half Asleep in Frog Pajamas*, for instance, which opens like this:

> The day the stock market falls out of bed and breaks its back is the worst day of your life. Or so you think. It isn't the worst day of your life, but you think it is. And when you give voice to that thought, it is with conviction and a minimum of rhetorical embellishment.

That kind of second-person point of view has been used—at least, in bits and pieces—by such literary masters as Camus, Fuentes, Hawthorne, Faulkner, and Grass, but it is unlikely that it will be used by you. If you did decide to give it a whirl, it would probably leave you feeling very detached from what you are seeking to portray, almost as if you were casting a clinical eye on your material. In fact, I think only an exceptionally unusual person would choose to convey his or her "last say" in such a detached and clinical way. Mr. Spock, perhaps?

Third Person

While a first-person voice can be very engaging for a reader, a third-person point of view is pretty much the default position in fiction. If you're a Bible reader, it's the point of view that you're used to:

> And the Lord God formed the rib which he had taken from the man into a woman, and brought her unto the man.

If you love Jackie Collins, that's also the point of view you've come to expect, as in the opening of *Chances*:

> Costa Zennocotti stared at the girl sitting across from him, his ornate carved wood desk separating them. She spoke rapidly, gesticulating wildly, making faces to emphasize a point. Christ! He hated himself for having such thoughts, but she was the most sensual woman he had ever laid eyes on . . .

Both the Bible and *Chances*—two works of literature that are about as far from each other as possible—are written in the third person.

Third-person narration can be *omniscient*—meaning that the narrator knows everything about everyone and can pop in and out of a character's head at will—or it can be limited, as in a third-person narration that closely follows the thoughts of only one character.

As with the second-person point of view, it is unlikely that you would choose to tell your story in a third-person voice. *Your* story will most likely sound best to *your* ears in *your* voice. But who knows? You can certainly experiment with voice, and I, for one, will give you props for trying. Maybe you'll tell two thirds of your "last say" in a third-person voice—portraying the 12-year-old boy you once were—and then, in the last third, you'll revert to your default first-person voice, for some reflection on that first section. That could be cool. Or it could be totally unsuccessful and you'll trash it. What's the harm? We're talking about a short piece of writing here. If you try something and it doesn't work, no one gets hurt. Just go back and try something else.

Note, too, that whichever point of view you choose to work with, you will still have all of the same narrative problems to address: "The Once," The Ordinary vs. The Extraordinary, Tension and Conflict, and The Point. Nothing about point of view changes as a result of those decisions.

TENSE

When you have resolved your "Person" point of view—at least in a way that feels good to you—that doesn't mean your problems are over. You then have to decide on the tense. The tense refers to the time frame in which the narrative unfolds. Once again, you have limited choices and these will always be the same: past, present, or future.

Past Tense

One day, when I was talking to my uncle, who had just turned 90, he told me that the older he gets, the more time he spends in the past. Instead of looking forward, he looks backward. I suppose this life review exercise that we are engaged in is another manifestation of the syndrome he was describing, but it's good to take that backward look while we can still think relatively clearly. Consequently, when you're telling your "last say," it's very likely that you're going to find yourself using the past tense. It just seems to come naturally.

You saw that I used the past tense in my essay about meeting my son at Grand Central Terminal. I'd like to go back to that essay for a moment, if you'll indulge me, and see what it might look like if I had chosen to tell it in the present tense.

There I stand, on the Main Concourse of Grand Central Terminal at the information booth, as planned, holding a bag of hot pretzels from Zaro's, looking around in every direction. It's Friday afternoon of a long summer weekend and everyone seems to have somewhere to get to. It occurs to me that Noah might be late, but then I see him, my son, coming toward me in the surge of people. Nineteen years old, baseball cap, tattered jeans, flip-flops, duffel bag, smile, wave, and off we go to board our train, finding seats that face the right way, and settling in for the two-hour trip to Wassaic, where we will pick up our car and drive the extra hour home.

Following the pretzels and a few perfunctory replies to my questions about his summer internship, Noah falls asleep. In that July heat, the drool collects at the corner of his shiny lip, just as it used to in his stroller. I kick off my shoes and look around at all the men in their summer gabardine suits, jackets folded and stashed away, ties loosened, laptops out. I close my eyes too, and then, in that damp half state between sleep and waking, my mind wanders to memories of my own father, a man in a gray flannel suit, who every now and then would take me to the city with him on the commuter train from Scarsdale. In such moments of rare, uncomfortable proximity, my father would attempt to instruct me in worldly skills, like the proper way to fold the *New York Times*. For my father, who based his life on mastering rituals, this action was as prescribed and formal as the folding of a military flag. I watched and ignored in equal measure. What have I taught my sons? I wonder, as I drift through the half-sleep.

Then there is a startling whistle and a few minutes before the train is due to arrive in Wassaic, Noah and I gather our things and stand in the aisle. Behind me, a man approximately my age is craning to look out the window and seems agitated. He asks me which station this is and when I tell him, he says that he slept right through Dover Plains, the station before, and doesn't know how he is going to get back to his car. As Dover Plains is only a few minutes' detour, I offer to drive him. Along the way, we chat. He tells us that he's a professor of art at Yale; I tell him I'm a writer. When we drop him off at his car, he thanks me profusely and says to Noah, "Your father is a gentleman."

Back on the road, heading north on 22, Noah and I drive in silence for a few miles. Finally, he speaks.

"Why did you do that?" he asks, with an edge of annoyance in his voice.

I know where the edge is coming from. He is challenging me to tell a truth and is wary that I might not produce one.

"You must always, always do the good thing," I say.

And that's enough. With a sideways glance, I see him thinking about it. Then he puts on a CD and for the rest of the trip home we listen to Dylan.

So what did you think? I rather like the present tense there, and although I hadn't thought to use it when I first wrote the piece, seeing it now makes me feel like it was something I should have considered. Of course, things change when you go from past tense to present tense. When you're in that past tense voice, a kind of elegiac quality can emerge. What do I mean by "elegiac"? A sense of mourning. In a piece like mine, I am celebrating a value—*always doing the good thing*—and re-creating a relationship with my son that has been central to my life. But when I tell a story in the past tense, something elegiac creeps in as well because I am mourning the passage of time. Well, friends, that elegiac quality is not inappropriate to this task we are taking on. This is, after all, our "last say" and, by extension, our last chance to make meaning of life. That is a heavy thing, even though it can also be a joyful and life-affirming thing. So most of us will not resist settling into that past tense.

There are ways, however, that we can ameliorate some of that past-tense feeling and introduce more of a present-feeling in a past-tense piece. Dialogue, for instance, can inject a more active feeling into a piece. When people talk to each other, the reader has the sense of something going on and that feels "present."

Some of us, however, may resist the past tense altogether. We will not go gently into that good night and may
feel more comfortable telling our story in the present tense.
We may want to keep alive the sense of ourselves as active
people—which, of course, we are—and that's absolutely
fine, too. It's really all about you—as a person, as a writer.
You determine the direction you go in with tense. And you
should also know that you can combine tenses. For instance,
you might start in the past tense but end your essay in the
present tense—that is, in the here and now as you reflect
on what you have shared. There are all kinds of ways that a
writer can play with tense.

Future Tense

As I've said, there are three options to choose from when it
comes to tense: past, present, and future. Future, you say?
Yes, that is a choice—but not really. I can't think of a writer
who has pulled off writing a sustained piece of fiction in
the future tense. It's quite unlikely that someone could—I
will go there; I *will* do that—even if you wanted to give
your piece a certain sci-fi flair. And certainly for your "last
say," when you're almost certainly going to be looking ret-
rospectively rather than forward, a future tense seems impossible. So let's not worry about that one.

NUMBER

Now that we've sorted out Person and Tense, we have one more point of view issue to resolve: Number. And here you have only two choices: singular or plural.

Singular

You are using a first-person singular point of view if you are the narrator and you are referring to yourself. Just to give you a break from my Grand Central Terminal piece, let's look back to a portion of Anne's essay to remind us what that first-person singular voice sounds like:

> I shape my lips into a round, "aw"-shaped smile and inhale deeply. All around me I hear the sound of circular breathing, feeling its warm and sustaining force. Justina, our director, nods, and we exhale the first chord of Cristóbal de Morales's "Alleluia." It's true, in sync, in tune. We're really together this afternoon.

As you can see, Anne is telling her story from the singular point of view. "*I* shape *my* lips into a round, 'aw'-shaped smile and inhale deeply." Now, just a little bit further down, she switches to a plural number, when she says,

"We're really together this afternoon," referring to her choral group. And that makes sense, because we are all individuals and yet we also make up many different groups.

As with "Person," your point of view choice here will most likely be fairly straightforward. Since this is *your* "last say," you will probably choose first-person singular to tell your story. And that's all well and good.

Plural

It's not inconceivable, however, that you would decide to tell your "last say" in a plural voice. Let's imagine, for instance, that the value you wanted to pass on to those you care about is teamwork. In order to do that, you choose a story about an experience in which you've been part of a group that has been very important in your life. This could be an athletic team or it could be a woodwind ensemble or a Navy SEALs outfit or a jury. If a pivotal moment of your life has taken place in such a group context, then it might work to tell your story from the plural point of view. Or you might tell two-thirds of it from a plural point of view, in the past, and then, let's say, shift to the singular first person in the present to reflect on the experience.

The exhilarating thing about writing is knowing that all of these options are open to you, free of charge. Your only investment is the time it takes to experiment. That expenditure of time can sometimes be frustrating, when you wind up in blind alleys, but it can just as well be stimulating, exciting, and rewarding. Committing yourself to some spirit of adventure when it comes to writing can turn an ordinary experience into a transformative one.

The Last Say: Alice

I was working with a woman who had enjoyed a very rich and satisfying life. Alice, who was in her early 70s, grew up on New York's Upper West Side in an artistic family. She got married at a young age to a brilliant engineer and they had three children. Alice had a whole mother lode of solid values to pass on to her kids and her grandkids and her extended family, to whom she was extremely close, and hence there was so much she could have written about. But one of the biggest themes in Alice's life was music and especially the teaching of music. Alice had taught music in her local public schools for many years, and so she decided to explore that facet of her identity in her "last say."

Alice had a pretty complicated story to tell, and so it took a fair amount of back-and-forth to get it right. One issue was that a lot of time was being covered. This was a "memory" piece that was quite layered in terms of time. It started out in Alice's relatively recent past, describing a reunion with a former student, which kicked off a memory from many years before of her interaction with her class, of which the former student was a member.

It is not easy in a short piece to handle shifts in time like that—and it wasn't especially easy for Alice to locate the heart of her story. What ultimately came forward as the story's core was Alice's feeling that teaching is a gift that goes back and forth between individuals. In this story, Alice and her former student Ryan exchange that gift, but the gift is also recalled in the influence that Alice felt from her encounter with a great teacher, the legendary Leonard Bernstein.

Let's have a look:

I was in my music classroom late one fall afternoon after the children had been dismissed. It was beginning to get dark and I was racing to turn in the first-quarter grades. It was taking me more time than I had planned and I was unaware that someone had walked into the room. "Hey, Mrs. Swersey? Remember me?"

I looked up and saw a tall, sandy-haired young man in a plaid flannel shirt and denim overalls. Ryan had been one of my students five years before. "Of course I remember you, Ryan," I said. "Although I didn't have to look up at you when I saw you last."

As we spoke, he told me that he was now in high school in the agricultural program in Northampton.

The school bus had dropped him off at the elementary school and he was waiting for his mother to pick him up.

"You know," Ryan said, as I watched him walk around the room inspecting the rhythm instruments on the shelves, "I'll never forget what you taught us about Leonard Bernstein."

One morning back in 1990, as I was driving to Berkshire Trail Elementary School in rural western Massachusetts, the news on the radio announced the death of Leonard Bernstein, the night before. I pulled the car over to the side of the road, turned off the engine, and wept. Bernstein had been my maestro. When I was in high school we often got special passes to attend Friday afternoon rehearsals at Carnegie Hall, where he was conducting the New York Philharmonic. When he noticed that a group of students were in the audience, he would sit down on the edge of the stage and talk to us about the music he was preparing. He was a master teacher and I always cherished how lucky I was to be one of his "students."

I had known that Bernstein was very ill. I had seen him conduct his next-to-last concert at Tanglewood two months before, visibly fragile, stooped over with a cape covering his shoulders on that warm August evening. After that concert I decided that I would teach my students about Leonard Bernstein, the man and his music.

I spent the last few weeks of summer preparing a six-week unit on Bernstein. I wanted the children in this part of the world, where Tanglewood rules in the summer, to know of the contribution Bernstein made to this venerable music festival, where he was a major presence for more than 40 years. Most of the children had never been to Tanglewood, but some knew of it because their parents worked there behind the scenes, collecting garbage and tending the grounds.

That year, when the school term started, my classroom was hung with photographs of the Maestro. We read that Bernstein, who became a musician over the objections of his father, had natural talent, and we began to learn parts of *West Side Story*. The morning I heard about Bernstein's death, I shared the news with my classes. The children were all very concerned, particularly since they observed my sadness. As a result of Bernstein's passing, children who could barely read brought in stories about him from *Time* and *Newsweek* magazines they found at their grandmother's or the dentist. The excitement in the music class was amplified by the coincidence of the death of the Maestro.

"Sometimes these days I listen to jazz and I kind of like it. Oh, there's my mom," said Ryan. "See you, Mrs. Swersey."

"See you, Ryan," I said, as he left the classroom.

You never know what kind of impact a teacher can

have on a child, I thought. As I remembered Bernstein for what he had taught me, one of my students remembered what I taught him. I was glad that I stayed late at school that day.

The other individuals that made up Alice's writing group were all quite moved by this piece. They had known that Alice taught music, but they didn't necessarily know how profoundly important it had been to her. This "last say" conveyed that, but it conveyed something else that was very important about Alice: the fact that she is somebody who cares deeply about people. That is a value in her life. And in this "last say" she showed herself as a person who was open to the many kinds of interactions that people can have with one another. In her "last say," she brought home the idea, in a graceful and affecting way, that we all have the potential to influence one another. That is a powerful value to convey, and, in capturing that value in an essay, Alice created an important keepsake for those who knew and cared about her.

CHAPTER 4

The First Draft

By now, we've examined the elements of the narrative, we've asked ourselves exploratory questions in order to locate a topic, and we've educated ourselves about point of view. Next, it's time to actually put pen to paper. (Finger to keyboard?) As I have already indicated, this is not an easy moment. Regardless of whether you are a great writer or just an average person, it can be hard to get going.

Different writers use different routines to help with their ignition. Dan Brown of *The Da Vinci Code* fame goes all out in the direction of discipline. He gets up every day at 4:00 a.m. and writes for 60-minute stints that are timed by an antique hourglass. Every hour on the hour, he does some sort of physical exercise. I'm not sure how many such stints he goes through on an average day, but the whole idea makes my stomach hurt. Truman Capote, on the other hand, would lie like an odalisque on a divan, sipping sherry or a martini, and write in longhand. Then there was Victor Hugo, whose unique approach to writing resulted in masterworks like *Les Misérables* and *The Hunchback of Notre Dame*. Given to procrastination, Hugo would instruct his valet to confiscate all of his clothes. Stark naked and therefore confined to his house, he had nothing to do but write. (And quite a constitution Hugo had, as the naked scribe managed to live to the ripe old age of 83, even in those drafty 19th-century homes.)

Before you get started with your first draft, you may also need to engage in certain collateral activities. And amid the pacing, ball bouncing, deep knee bends, and coffee drinking (or sherry sipping), you might want to try some limbering exercises for the mind.

FREEWRITING

Many people look back at their early writing experiences with deep dread. All they can remember are a lot of *don't*s. *Don't* start a sentence with a conjunction. (And a conjunction is what again?) *Don't* end a sentence with a preposition. (And a preposition is what again?) Our goal is to free you of such rules so that you can actually get some writing done. After all, writing is hard enough without having to worry about the rules. It is, by its very nature, a challenging experience, no matter what your level of expertise may be. Writing is about trying to execute one's vision—and any writer can tell you that vision and execution can be (and can remain) poles apart.

In the many years that I have toiled as a professional writer, I cannot tell you how many times I went to bed at night, thinking that what I had written was exactly as it should be, only to awaken in the morning to find that the prose, and even the concept behind it, had evaporated. Oh yes, the words were still there on the paper, but the *meaning* behind the words, and all the attendant energy, had disappeared.

It is important to remember that perfection does not exist in writing. Some works come very close—*Madame Bovary, The Great Gatsby, Hamlet*—but I would wager that those works always felt somehow imperfect to their creators, who must have seen things that they wished they could have made a little better. There can be a perfect square, a perfectly pitched baseball game, a perfect hard-boiled egg, but perfect writing? I think not.

The process of bringing vision and execution into some kind of alignment is called drafting. And if you've been away from writing for a while, you may not recall that much about drafting. Drafting is essentially rewriting, which, for me, anyway, has become the real joy of writing. I love the act of taking something shapeless—those first drafts—and giving them shape. And I'm not alone in this.

Truman Capote, that sherry-sipping fellow who wrote supine on divans, once said, "Writing is rewriting." And William Zinsser, author of the legendary writing bible *On Writing Well*, stated, "Rewriting is the essence of writing well—where the game is won or lost."

For our purposes, let's anticipate that your piece will go through at least three drafts and a polish. Now that's not to say that you might not go through eight drafts. This happens—and there is no problem with that. Exertion, frustration, and even, on occasion, anguish, but no problem. You have to understand that there are no assurances when you go into a piece of writing—it's always uncharted territory, with each piece following its own pattern—and so there is no shame in getting lost. If a piece takes eight or nine or ten or twenty drafts to get it right, that's just the way it is. Of course, there are some pieces that are never going to pan out, and then we have to cut our losses and move on. You'll know when that happens. As we move along in this book, you'll learn how to judge when it's time to move from one draft to another—and when, disappointingly, it's time to call it quits on a certain piece. For now, however, we're still talking about getting started. And that brings us to freewriting.

Freewriting is a powerful procrastination buster and a valuable mental exercise that can help get your writing juices flowing. When you freewrite, all rules and regulations go out the window. You simply set aside a prescribed amount of time—ten minutes feels good—to *just write*. If you're doing this preparatory to writing a "last say," keep in mind that your freewriting doesn't have to have a thing to do with what you ultimately wind up writing. It could be about bread baking or kangaroos or the wart you just found on your thumb. Anything and everything that comes into your mind and asks to be written is welcomed. And when you're freewriting, you're not going to concern yourself with spelling, punctuation, syntax, tense, word choice, or anything like that. You don't worry about what you're writing and you certainly don't criticize yourself. You just let the writing happen for the set amount of time, and, when the time is up, you look to see what you've produced. And, again, whatever you've produced is just fine. When it comes to freewriting, there is no good, better, best—or bad, worse, worst. No judgments and no agenda. It is what it is.

Whenever I ask a group to engage in freewriting, there is usually a stunned silence. For most people, it simply doesn't feel right to write without rules because we have generally been reared to think that writing is all *about* rules. In truth, there *are* a great many rules around writing. You can't just drop a period into the middle of a sentence, for instance, because then you'll have two sentences and, not only that, but also one or the other of those sentences might lack a subject or a predicate. (Think noun and verb.) But before we worry about rules, we have to get something down on paper, and freewriting can help open up the sluice gates.

Once the group gets past the stunned silence that invariably accompanies the prescribed freewriting, some may ask questions and voice concerns. Fair enough. Then I set the timer for ten minutes, and, during that time, some folks engage in what might be called resistance. I've had students, for instance, who have spent the entire ten minutes writing *This is stupid* over and over and over again. That's entirely their prerogative, however; indeed, by the standards of freewriting, they are very much within their rights to be doing just that and, in so doing, might be throwing off some shackles.

So then, when you're getting ready to write your first draft, you might want to try this freewriting exercise. All that is required is a writing implement, something to write on, and ten minutes of your time. When you're finished, you'll look over what you've written and who knows? Maybe you'll find some valuable seeds for future writing exploration. Perhaps a certain phrase will arrest your attention or a metaphor will capture your interest. Even one good word can do a lot to send you in a fruitful direction. But even if nothing concrete comes of this exercise, the calisthenic nature of the freewriting still renders it worthwhile.

Keep in mind, too, that while I am suggesting you try freewriting at the start of your writing project, you can always go back to it whenever the mood—or the need—strikes you. Why not freewrite *between* drafts? After all, there is certainly a risk of getting clogged up between drafts, particularly when the drafts are allowed to sit around too long. Going back to freewriting could be a way to snake out those clogged passages and get the process flowing again.

P.S. AN IDEA

I want to pass along a little trick of the trade that I've used with my high school students—a neat way to pull a fast one on yourself when you're dragging your feet. Start your first draft by writing it as if you were writing a letter to a friend.

Those of us who are not 17 years old (or even close) can actually remember what it felt like to write a letter, and, for our population, this harmless illusion could really turn the tide if we're feeling stuck. (With my 17-year-olds, I suggest they try to do this exercise as an e-mail. Many of them, however, have never even written e-mails, and texting just won't work for this.)

The conversational nature of epistolary writing can help loosen you up enough so that you can produce a good amount of prose that can then be trimmed, massaged, and reworked as necessary. Now, if you were one of those kids who balked at writing letters home from camp, then this might not be the exercise for you. But, if at any point in your life, you have enjoyed writing letters, this is the time to re-call that pleasure—and to let it move you into your first draft.

AND SO IT BEGINS . . .

OK. You've done your freewriting (or not). You've tricked your mind with the letter-writing gambit (or not). Now comes the time for drafting.

You remember that we were discussing drafting as a way of bringing vision and execution into alignment. As an overview, here is what your drafting process might look like:

- Your first draft is going to be about getting it down on paper. Once it's there, you look it over, shake your head, figure out what works and what doesn't, and move on to the second draft.
- In the second draft, you might decide to substan-tially reorganize the chronology of your narra-tive. Maybe you'll choose to start in the middle and go back to the beginning as the piece pro-gresses. Maybe you'll cut out whole sections be-

cause, even though they're colorful and well told, they aren't really serving the overall objective of the essay. Maybe you'll start to wonder why a certain section is there at all, but as you dig deeper, you'll uncover new layers of meaning.

- By the time you reach your third draft, you'll be concentrating on issues of style. Is your voice original and compelling? Is your tone too flip or too dry? Are there better ways to say what you're trying to say? Stick with this intense examination. Take yourself to a quiet place and allow yourself to hear your authentic voice.

- Once you've arrived at the final polish stage, you'll be looking at every comma, seeing whether there are any extraneous words to cut, making sure that all of your subjects and verbs agree— that sort of thing.

Now keep in mind that I'm talking generally here about three drafts and a polish, but the only thing that is really sure about writing is that there are no assurances. A piece that seems like it should be simple could wind up taking five drafts to get just right. By the same token, you might nail a more complex piece and be out the door in three drafts. Just know that there is no stigma to more drafts. A piece requires as many drafts as it requires, and you'll have to make allowances for that.

TAKE IT FROM THE TOP

Beginnings (and endings) are very often the hardest part to get right in a piece of writing. Your first draft has to start somewhere, and locating that "somewhere," if you recall, is your first problem to solve ("The Once"). We have to situate the story in time and we have to remember that we don't have all the time in the world. In fact, you only have between 500 and 1,000 words, as that is the word limit that we set for ourselves, thinking that was about as much as most people would feel comfortable receiving through an oral presentation.

Let's look at this process through the lens of my friend Anne's essay (the choir one). Here is how Anne started out her first draft:

> The small New England church is already full as we take our places at the front. It's deep winter, and the nine of us are swathed in sweaters and scarves—and close-fitting hats in solidarity with Laurel, our soprano soloist, a recent cancer survivor. We're all in various stages of middle age, and we're all busy with our lives, but not even the snow could keep our committed little group from singing.
>
> The piano offers the first notes of Cristóbal de Morales's "Alleluia." I shape my lips into a round, "aw"-

shaped smile and inhale. All around me I hear the sound of circular breathing, feeling its warm and sustaining force. Justina, our director, nods, and we exhale the first chord. It's true, in sync, in tune. It sounds beautiful—a great beginning to our recital.

When Anne sat down to write her first draft, she did so with good instincts. She knew that she wasn't going to start this story in her driveway, in the Stop and Shop, at the breakfast table . . . no. She knew she had to get into the story relatively quickly. The opening she chose in her first draft was by no means a bad one, but here is how the opening read in her finished piece:

I shape my lips into a round, "aw"-shaped smile and inhale deeply. All around me I hear the sound of circular breathing, feeling its warm and sustaining force. Justina, our director, nods, and we exhale the first chord of Cristóbal de Morales's "Alleluia." It's true, in sync, in tune. We're really together this afternoon.

It's deep winter, and the audience that fills this small drafty New England church is swathed in sweaters and scarves. We nine singers are also wearing close-fitting hats in solidarity with Laurel, our soprano soloist, a recent cancer survivor. We're all in various stages of middle age, busy with our lives, but not even a blizzard could keep us away from this recital.

There is often some value to be found in not being quite so linear with your narrative. So, as you can see, Anne's final version focuses on that "aw" action in the beginning, stimulating readers to find out what that might mean, and then pulls back to situate the action in a larger context.

Often, I find myself counseling the writers I'm working with to lop off their first couple of paragraphs altogether. These are very likely to be backstory—that is, facts about how you arrived at the beginning of your story. In Anne's case, such verbiage might conceivably have sounded like this:

> I've always loved to sing and have been in choirs on and off for most of my adult life. Not only do I love the music, but I relish the camaraderie that comes with this activity.

These are nice sentiments, which can *inform* the writing, but they are not needed at the beginning of the narrative when you're looking to make the most of your time.

A particularly useful literary device for getting into a short piece like this is called in medias res—Latin for "in the middle of things"—which plunges the reader into the action:

- The current took hold of me.
- The car swerved wildly.
- "Stop!" I said. "This has gone far enough."

Openings such as these can't help but grab your attention, which obviously is a very good thing at the beginning of a piece. Some people might find such openings a tad corny, and, in all honesty, they can be a tad corny, but if the general level of the writing is where it should be, very few readers will hold against you a literary device that might be slightly hoary. The in medias res openings such as those above clearly trump beginnings like these:

- I don't know where to begin, so let's begin at the beginning.
- I have always been fascinated by nature. Seeing God's design in even the smallest leaf or tiniest bug is, to me, an extraordinary thing. That is why, when I went to Costa Rica, I was in heaven.
- Count Leo Tolstoy famously wrote that "all happy families are alike; each unhappy family is unhappy in its own way."

If you look at those three openings, you'll see that the first one serves absolutely no purpose and so off goes its head. The second feels like padding, and even if such sentiments are important to you—talking about "God's design," for instance—you can probably find some other place in your essay to put that, just not at the beginning when you're eager to form a relationship with your reader. As to the third, I would say that it is highly inadvisable to start your "last say" with a quotation. Toastmasters International might sanction such an approach, but for this occasion, you really want to focus on your own thoughts and feelings, not Count Leo Tolstoy's, Dorothy Parker's, or Stephen Colbert's.

A great first sentence can certainly help anchor a piece—or even an entire novel (*Call Me Ishmael. I am an invisible man. All boys, except for one, grow up.*). But the chances of your coming up with a great first sentence right off the bat are, in a word, remote. So by no means should you get hung up on that issue.

What will actually signify the real beginning of your writing is that unmistakable feeling of exploration that accompanies creation. If you can just allow yourself to write, without censoring yourself or setting unreal expectations, then you can start doing the work that you are supposed to be doing in your first draft. And if that work is coming very slowly—if procrastination is taking its toll—then use a few tried-and-true methods to trick that old devil. One nice ruse is to set a quota. Sometimes I'll tell myself that I cannot stop working until I produce 300 or 500 or 800 words that day. (The actual word count is dictated by any number of variables, such as the complexity of the work, the other pursuits in my life that are competing for my attention, my general energy level, and so forth.) It works for me—and could for you.

Once you understand that your goal in the first draft is to simply get down words and amass raw material that can be shaped over a succession of drafts, then you can lower the bar you have set for yourself. You will understand that this first-draft experience might be a bit scary, but it's only part of a process. In fact, it is not in the least bit unusual for a third draft to bear very little resemblance to a first draft. A great deal can change from draft to draft, but nothing will change, or even happen, if you can't manage to get that first draft down. So your piece happens to be too long—so what? So it doesn't move, it's full of loose ends and blind alleys—big deal. So it's fuzzy and dense at the same time. Don't worry about it. That's what first drafts are all about.

I often suggest to my 17- and 18-year-old writers that they not even try to make their first drafts especially good. So many of these students are so driven. They have perfect averages, perfect test scores, and somehow they think that their first drafts can be perfect as well. Sorry, overachievers, but it is absolutely in the nature of a first draft to be *imperfect*. Indeed, the challenge at the first-draft stage is to not get hung up on that imperfection but to sit with it, to *be* with it. You need to see the problems in the work, calmly and clearly, and then soldier on.

Interestingly, I have found that my adult writers are often as intense about the work as these kids who are stepping over one another to get into the best colleges. Where does that intensity come from for the adult writers? As I see it, it comes from the need to *make meaning of one's life*. At a certain point, there is obviously less time than there used to be, and the wish to make the most of that time in order to gain clarity on what our lives have been about can feel like a real pressure.

"BIG PICTURE" EDITING

OK. Let's assume that you've overcome your initial resistance and you've managed to get a draft down on paper. The first thing to do is read it out loud. I always urge my high school seniors to read their college admissions essays out loud. I promise them that their ears will pick up problems that have escaped their eyes. The same applies to you. Reading your drafts out loud is especially important in terms of this assignment, as the presumption is that your "last say" may one day be delivered orally. You want to make sure that a speaker will be able to easily say your words. You certainly don't want that speaker to get mired in sticky prose while your message gets mangled.

Good writing is very much about achieving a satisfying rhythm, not just from sentence to sentence but from paragraph to paragraph and also within the internal structure of each discrete sentence. I like to think of every sentence I write as a wave that builds up momentum as it goes along and then breaks in the spot that feels most natural and right, pulling back out to sea to make way for a new sentence.

As I've suggested, you can best hear the internal

rhythm of your sentences by speaking each one aloud. In doing so, you run a good chance of spotting those repetitive sentence structures, dull repetition of words, tangles in which nouns and verbs do not agree, weak passive constructions into which you may have lapsed, and other such common failings. Even though I turn out hundreds of words a day for my work, I still take the time to read those words out loud so that my ear can catch what my eye might miss. I wouldn't know how to do it any other way.

I counsel my 17- and 18-year-old writers to repair to a quiet place to read their work. Many of them are so attached to their cell phones that they hardly ever experience real quiet and are afraid of it. I have to say that the same seems to hold true for most of us these days. We are all subject to the electronic buzz that surrounds us—phone, Internet, TV, radio, 24-hour news cycle—and the point at which you will be reading and sitting with your first draft is an opportune occasion to *just say no.* Turn it all off, go to the park, the rooftop, the library, a cemetery (I have often worked in those silent, stately places), and allow yourself to hear your words and your voice. Your goal is to capture the essence that is specific to you and get it down on paper. And in order to do that, you have to hear yourself.

When you've read the first draft—out loud—chances are that just about everything in it may strike you as disjointed, disconnected, and downright dismaying. *Why am I doing this?* you ask yourself. *Shouldn't I be going out for brunch?* This is not the time, however, to throw it all over for that plate of eggs Benedict. This is the time to double down and carry on with the work.

One way you can help yourself is by actively suspending judgment. If you look carefully and calmly at what you've written, you'll probably find something to like in this first draft. A paragraph, a sentence, an expression, a word—find it and use it as a life preserver to hold on to. Remind yourself, too, that every other writer has toiled in these trenches. Have a look at a draft from Charles Dickens's *Great Expectations*:

Now that turned out to be a pretty good book, didn't it?

And, unlike Dickens, we have cut and paste available to us.

Generally speaking, it's important that you hold nothing sacred at this stage—or at any other stage of the drafting process. A famous adage in literary circles states that writing is all about "killing your babies." There seems to be no definitive attribution, but if you Google around, you'll sometimes find it attributed to William Faulkner, who is quoted as having said, "In writing, you must kill all your darlings." (So sometimes you'll see the expression stated as: *kill your darlings*.) In any case, what it means—and what must not be forgotten—is that nothing is so precious in writing that it can't be eliminated *if it doesn't serve the overriding concept of the piece*. This pertains to delicious phrases, delightful metaphors, divine anecdotes, and de-lovely words. They must all go into the trash, no matter how much you love them, if they don't feed into that overriding concept of the piece. And believe me—as the father of two beloved sons and now two delicious, delightful, de-lovely grandchildren, I don't say *Kill your babies* lightly. But I've been in the writing game long enough to know that this is an absolutely critical piece of advice.

PLENTY OF PITFALLS

So, in reading this first draft, you will see many things wrong. As I say, that's a dime-a-dozen experience when it comes to first drafts. I'd like to take a moment now to go over some of the ways that good essays can go bad.

Concept

The best execution in the world won't count for anything if your concept is just plain wrong. Let's imagine, for instance, that you thought it would be clever and very much like you (a clever, prankster sort of person) to write your "last say" as your obituary . . . but in pig Latin. It seemed to you a wonderfully irreverent tour de force. But when you tried it out on your wife and then on your brother and then on your best friend, you noticed that they all began to glaze over after the first sentence. Yes, it's true—pig Latin has that effect on people. So as cleverly as you may have spun your porcine prose, the fact is that your concept was way off base.

Now that's a fairly extreme example of how a piece of writing can fail on concept. More likely, a conceptual failure will be one that has presented itself as being too predictable, too familiar, too large in scope for the allotted length, or too small in scope to be played out in that length. If you suffer a conceptual failure, then the best advice is probably to put that concept aside and go for another one. After all, we're not talking about a novel here (though novels certainly suffer from conceptual misfires as well). We're talking about a 500- to 1,000-word essay.

Presentation

Now let's assume that your concept is just fine but your presentation left something to be desired. Perhaps you got lost in your run-on sentences and what you wrote came out as a syntactical quagmire. Maybe you thought that the key to bringing your concept to life was to use as many big words as you could: *magnanimous, pusillanimous, choleric, antediluvian.* Well, who talks like that and who wants to listen to something that thesaurus driven? Or maybe you relied on clichés to carry your piece along, or went overboard with description, oozing metaphors from every pore.

The good news is that compared with conceptual problems, problems that have to do with presentation are often remediable. In fact, sometimes the fixes around such issues are fast and easy. (Prone to clichés? Go through your piece either by yourself or with someone's help and shear away that flab.) Let's compare it to a dress, for instance. If a dress is really well constructed, then the pom-poms and bows and gewgaws that are bringing down its level of tastefulness can be snipped away to reveal those good lines. No need to get rid of a whole outfit when some simple nips and tucks can take care of the problem.

Structure

A faulty structure is a technical problem that often shows itself in the first or even second draft (sometimes later still), but, again, not to despair, for such problems can usually be fixed.

Read your draft carefully and see if you successfully devised a sound structure that you were able to sustain over the course of your piece. Does the piece flow? Or does it stop and start and stop and start? Did you spend too much time setting up the situation and then had to play catch-up to bring the piece to a close? Does your middle section feel baggy and overblown? If yes to any of the above, then your reader—in this case, you—will come away feeling unsatisfied, as if there hasn't been enough to eat on the plate. One way to gain insight into the structure of your piece is to actually outline your finished draft. When you look at it in that skeletal form, the structural flaws might pop out for you. Maybe you'll want to put the beginning at the end or something similarly radical. Those kinds of solutions can often work.

Tone

In addition to flaws in your concept, problems with your presentation, and any structural deficiencies that might be lurking, your draft can also be suffering from egregious lapses in tone.

Since so many people approach writing with some trepidation, it's natural to assume that their tone, when they take on a writing project like this, could be shaky. You might, for instance, be assuming a tone that is overly formal, when what you really want to aspire to is a natural tone, in your own authentic voice. You have to be able to hear that voice, however.

An even bigger problem is that we live in an age, too, that can sometimes seem antithetical to good writing. Surrounded as we are by eduspeak and psychobabble and all those other ghastly jargons, it's hard to keep them out of our writing. The effects of such jargon on your "last say" could be quite dire, as this kind of language totally undercuts the presentation of your authentic voice that is so necessary to make the emotional connection you're aiming to attain with your reader/listener. We'll talk a little more about jargon—how to identify it and how to avoid it—later in the book.

Let's turn our attention now to our next "last say." This time, if you don't mind, I'd like to show you how that piece evolved—from first to second to third draft.

The Last Say: Steve   Steve, sixty-seven, had been through some tough times in recent years. His wife had been battling Stage IV cancer for almost a decade. During that time, Steve had made a career change into the field of nonprofit fundraising, and though he enjoyed his work, it was also quite stressful. Weighing his options, he decided that it would make sense for him to retire.

Steve had a healthy share of interests to keep him busy. He found great expression and release in physical activity. He loved to play tennis, practice yoga, and he especially loved to dance. He was also a fluent Spanish speaker, having spent time in South America in the Peace Corps, and he tutored in Spanish as well as English for Spanish speakers who were learning English as a second language. Another of his most prized activities was teaching a yoga dance class in New York City to cancer survivors.

Steve and I went back and forth on a writing topic. Initially, he thought he would do something about teaching

English to Spanish speakers, which I thought had good potential, but then he sent me the following e-mail:

> Now that I look at it, it occurs to me that there is another essay idea that interests me even more: namely, how my mother taught me to dance in a canteen in a bungalow colony when I was seven, how I saw her come alive at bar mitzvahs and weddings, dancing to Greek music and having men putting dollar bills on her forehead, and how that love of dance was transmitted to me so that I now teach Yoga Dance.

Well, naturally when I read this, I flipped for it. Dancing in the canteen of a bungalow colony? Dollar bills on the forehead? I was there! Seriously, people sometimes wonder how I can tell if an essay topic has real potential and, for me, it's pretty intuitive. I often rely on the little-hairs-on-the-back-of-my-neck system. That is to say, when those little hairs stick up, I know there is gold in them thar hills.

Steve went right to work and, before long, he produced a first draft. Please bear with me and have a look at these first, second, and third drafts of Steve's work, because I'd like you to get some sense of what drafting is all about. To that end, I am inserting comments in these drafts in bold type, so you can see how we move a piece like this along.

First Draft

Right-two-three-tap. With both hands over my head and pointing to the right, I'm leading a dance class to the sound of Selena's "Baila Esta Cumbia."

Left-two-three-tap. [**So far, so good. Steve gets us right into the action; it is economical and lively.**]

We're in Gilda's Club in downtown Manhattan. I come here every two weeks to lead a 90-minute "Yoga Dance" class for a group of women who are cancer survivors. I've been volunteering almost two years—a journey for me and my students, many who have been with me practically from the beginning. [**From here, until the end of this paragraph, it's starting to feel digressive and off point.**] Some have dropped out, and I fear that it's because they have passed away, because none of my regulars would miss a class. They love Yoga Dance—a form invented at Kripalu, the yoga center near our weekend home in Stockbridge. On Saturdays at Kripalu, the Yoga Dance is backed by African drums, and one of the instructors, noting that I was often the only one among the students who could actually do African dance steps, invited me to lead. Eventually, she asked me to assist her in a teacher-training program.

Left foot forward, right in place, left-right-left; right foot back, left in place, right-left-right.

After several false starts over several years because of my wife's cancer, I finally made it in October of 2010, just before retiring, and within a couple of months, I was at my first (and really only) gig, Gilda's Club. I'm pleased that quite a number of them couldn't dance, let alone do this step but now can. [**The main problem with this paragraph is that her cancer is coming in as a non sequitur.**]

Dancing with these women brings me back somehow to Swann Lake Bungalow Colony, a summer retreat about 50 miles north of New York City where my family escaped from the Bronx for a few weeks in the summer. My mother and I are in the canteen, which doubles or triples as a restaurant, soda fountain, and dance and event hall with a jukebox, and we're practicing the cha-cha, which was all the rage then.

Left foot forward, right in place . . .

"That's all there is to it, Steven," my mother says with a smile. "Really. You've got it."

We must look pretty cute. I am about seven and only come up to my mother's waist, but I have my hands around her in proper dance form and hers are resting on my shoulders. I can feel a sense of pride, joy, and mastery, which doesn't come easily to me at that stage of my life. I am still not quite over a 12-foot fall from a wall in a playground in the Bronx that resulted in a fractured hip and 10 weeks in traction in a hospital with the prognosis that I might never walk again. This trauma was followed by moving from my beloved grandparents' apartment to Sedgwick Project a half mile away, where I suddenly found myself embedded in a mini-gang of kids, all older and bigger and more physically adept than I, so that I often was not up to their level and left out. Here, at the canteen, it's really nice to feel this sense of mastery dancing the cha-cha and the fox-trot too.

I can also sense the transformation that dancing brings to my mother. Betty Kerner, née Rebecca Azaria, is a diffident, quiet, unassuming woman who takes care of my brother Howard and me. I think she generally didn't feel much gusto in her life as she was often physically not well from her early teenage years onward. She seemed to relate to her life as drudgery—one chore after another—whether it was doing the laundry or cleaning our apartment. [**The issue of drudgery here seems vague, cloudy.**] Over the years, my mother's energy and her persona slowly faded with her illnesses, but the one time she came alive was at bar mitzvahs and weddings. She just loved to dance.

Whenever the bands at the bar mitzvahs and weddings played the Middle Eastern music that evoke my mother's Sephardic background, I watched her slowly rise up to the dance floor and, out of I don't know where, she would start to do a Bronx version, but a very good one, mind you, of a belly dance. She wore a wonderful smile from head to foot as her body threw off its usual constraints. Although I didn't like the expression on men's faces as they placed dollar bills on the beads of sweat that covered my mother's joyful face, [**Need to fix that image. You can't put dollar bills on beads of sweat.**] I was so excited to see her displaying a side of herself that I and others rarely got to see.

Right-left-right-tap, left-right-left-tap.

I pull out of the memory and see my Gilda's ladies smiling and following my steps. I feel content. [**The big problem here? What is The Point?**]

Certainly there are things that need fixing here, but all in all, it's quite a good first draft. Let's have another look and see what kinds of changes Steve made in the second draft.

Second Draft

Right-two-three-tap. With both hands over my head, pointing to the right, I'm leading a dance class to the sounds of Selena's "Baila Esta Cumbia."

Left-two-three-tap.

I am here in Gilda's Club in downtown Manhattan, where I teach a 90-minute Yoga Dance Class every two weeks to a group of women who are, like my wife, cancer survivors. I've been volunteering almost two years—a journey for both me and my students, many who have been with me practically from the beginning. They love Yoga Dance, which I discovered at Kripalu, the yoga center near our weekend home in Stockbridge, where this form was invented.

Left foot forward, right in place, left-right-left . . .

Tonight, as I'm leading the women at Gilda's Club, I'm brought back to Wonder Lake Bungalow Colony, a summer retreat about 50 miles north of New York City. It was here that our family escaped from the sweltering heat of the Bronx for a few weeks every summer. Wonder meant lake swimming and sports for kids during the day, but things got pretty boring on weekday evenings when all the men were in the city working. One night, I was complaining about the lack of stuff to do and my mother said, "OK! Let's go down to the canteen and I'll teach you to dance."

Left foot forward, right in place.

The canteen doubled or tripled as a restaurant, soda fountain, and dance hall with a jukebox. There were people scattered around when my mother put on a cha-cha song that was the rage then, "Sweet and Gentle." We must have cut a cute scene. I was about seven and only came up to my mother's waist, but I had my hands around her in proper dance form. I recall how quickly I mastered the cha-cha, and how people were watching us and smiling. "That's all there is to it, Steven," my mother said, and she smiled such a happy smile—a sweet and gentle smile—and I remember feeling a sense of pride, joy, and mastery, which didn't come easily to me at that stage of my life.

Left foot forward, right in place.

I remember, too, how thrilled I felt to see that I had pleased my mother by learning to dance. Betty Kerner, born Rebecca Azaria, was a diffident, quiet, unassuming woman who took care of my younger brother Howard and me. I think she generally didn't feel much gusto in her life, as she was often physically not well from early teenage years onward. She seemed to relate to housekeeping as tiresome and drudgery—whether it was doing the laundry or cleaning our apartment. Over the years, my mother's energy and her persona slowly faded with her illnesses, but the one time she came alive was dancing at bar mitzvahs and weddings. She just loved to dance.

Whenever the bands would play the Middle Eastern music that recalled my mother's Sephardic background, I would watch her slowly rise up to the dance floor and, out of I don't know where, she would start to do a Bronx version, but a very good one, of a belly dance, with a wonderful smile from head to foot as her body threw off its usual constraints. Men—relatives and family friends—would affix dollar bills to the beads of sweat that covered her forehead and joyful face. I was excited and proud to see her displaying a side of herself that was rarely seen.

Right-left-right-tap, left-right-left-tap.

In these years when I too have sometimes felt a lack of gusto—heavy with the weight of living with illness—I, like my mother, find escape and meaning in the joy of physical movement, especially dance. As I _____ [somehow evoking more movement], I glance back over my shoulder and see that my Gilda ladies are smiling, sweet and gently, as they follow my steps. **[I offered Steve this last paragraph as a suggestion—a way to start connecting his memory to his current life. The blank in that last sentence is just a placeholder, I told him. Fill it in, change the language, make the language yours.]**

As you can see, the real problems that are left to address in this second draft are, for the most part, connected to The Point. Why is Steve asking the reader to read this? What does he want people to know about him? Let's see how he resolved that issue.

Third Draft

Right-left-one two-three. My hand, raised high, signals to start by bringing our right foot back. I'm leading a dance class to the tune of Alan Dale's famous 1955 cha-cha, "Sweet and Gentle." **[Did you notice that Steve changed the song in this draft? He wanted to evoke the music that was playing back in the bungalow colony.]**

Left-right-one-two-three.

We're here in Gilda's Club in downtown Manhattan, where I teach a 90-minute Yoga Dance Class every two weeks to a group of women who are, like my wife, cancer survivors. I've been volunteering for almost two years—a journey for me as well as my students, many who have been with me from the beginning. They love Yoga Dance, which I discovered at Kripalu, the yoga center near our weekend home in Stockbridge, where this dance form was invented.

Right-left-one-two-three.

Today, as I'm leading the class, I flash back to the Wonder Lake Bungalow Colony, a retreat about 50 miles north of New York City. It was here that our family escaped the sweltering heat of the Bronx for a few weeks in the summer. Wonder Lake meant swimming and sports during the day, but things got pretty boring on weekday evenings when all the husbands/fathers were in the city working. One night, I was complaining about the lack of things to do, and my mother, tired of hearing me, said, "OK! Let's go down to the canteen and I'll teach you to dance." That sounded real exciting to me!

Left-right-one-two-three.

The canteen doubled or tripled as a restaurant, soda fountain, and dance hall with a jukebox. There were people scattered around when my mother put on the cha-cha song that was the rage then, "Sweet and Gentle." We must have cut a cute scene. I was about eight and only came up to my mother's waist, but I had my hands around her, in proper dance form, as she instructed me. I recall how quickly I mastered the cha-cha, forward left-right-left-one-two-three, back right-left-one-two-three, and how people were watching us and smiling. "That's all there is to it, Steven," my mother said, and she smiled such a happy smile—a sweet and gentle smile. I remember feeling a sense of pride, joy, and mastery, which didn't come easily to me at that stage of my life.

Right-left-one-two-three.

I remember also how thrilled I felt to know that I had pleased my mother by learning to dance. Betty Kerner, born Rebecca Azaria, was a diffident, quiet, unassuming woman who took care of my younger brother Howard and me. I think she generally didn't feel much gusto in her life, as she was often physically not well from her teenage years onward. She seemed to relate to housekeeping as tiresome and drudgery—whether it was doing the laundry, cleaning our apartment, or even cooking. Over the years, my mother's energy and her persona slowly faded with her illnesses, but the one time she came alive was dancing at bar mitzvahs and weddings. She just loved to dance.

Whenever the band would play the Middle Eastern music that recalled my mother's Sephardic roots, I would watch her slowly rise up to the dance floor and, out of I don't know where, she would start to do a Bronx version, but a very good one, of a belly dance, with a wonderful smile from head to foot as she threw off her usual constraints. Men—relatives and family friends—would affix dollar bills to the beads of sweat that covered her forehead and joyful face. I was excited and proud to see her willing to make a public statement for herself, a side of my mother that was rarely seen.

Left-right-one-two-three.

In these last years when I, too, have sometimes felt a lack of gusto—exhausted with the weight of working in fundraising and living with my wife's illness—I, like my mother, find escape and meaning in the joy of physical movement, especially dance. I reflect on the importance of having a pastime that both enriches and balances, and have come to realize that sometimes it is only later in life that we recognize some treasure of learning that we received from our parents. Meanwhile, I glance back over my shoulder and see that my Gilda ladies are smiling, sweetly and gently, as they follow my steps.

By the time Steve finished his third draft, both he and I felt truly satisfied with the work. His "last say" emerged as a valuable and touching slice of family history. It sensitively evoked his ambivalent relationship with his mother but also became an affirmation of life, with dancing as the metaphor for the life force (which is generally what dancing is). Steve's excellent work was a validation of my hairs-on-the-back-of-my-neck meter. My instincts—and Steve's—were right on target.

Now please understand that many drafts go through far more changes than what you have seen here. In fact, when I work with writers and return their first drafts to them, it is not unusual for those drafts to be almost entirely covered by red. This is not something to despair over, I assure them. Indeed, when I send something to an editor, as I did with this book, I get something back that is similarly screaming red. For now, however, I did not wish to overwhelm you and so chose an essay that went through a much easier process.

All right, then—on to the second draft.

CHAPTER 5

The Second Draft

Having worked with a great many student writers, both 17- and 18-year-olds as well as those thoroughly mature individuals who are my contemporaries, it's hard to say where I've seen more fear: around the first or second draft. The first draft involves staring at a blank slate and experiencing all the anxiety that can be stirred up by such a sight. The second draft is about coming face-to-face with the shortcomings of your first draft and recognizing the difficulties you've had in aligning your vision and execution.

Both are bad . . . but, hey, that's the business of writing.

So there you are, looking at your next draft (imagine yourself as Dashiell Hammett, with an ashtray full of cigarette butts, a bottle of rye, and a fedora on your head). The thing is not working. What to do?

Look sharp, folks. The Avenue of Alteration lies ahead.

DRAFT TO DRAFT TO DRAFT . . .

If your first draft is not what you had hoped it would be, you have to start diagnosing the problems. We talked about basic conceptual problems and issues of tone. There can also be problems that have to do with identifying the Conflict. Perhaps, when you look at your draft, you're not sure what the blasted thing is *about*. Well, the problem may be that your piece isn't *about* anything yet. Perhaps the Conflict hasn't set in, or maybe you're not even sure what the Conflict is. This is the time to ask yourself precisely that question: *what is your essay about?*

I have seen short pieces that started with illness, continued on to career problems, and ended with marital strife. Oh, there was Conflict a-plenty, but Conflict should not mean a litany of woes. Conflict means, in the literary sense (and yes—you're writing literature), an incompatibility between characters or forces. In my piece about the train ride with my son, the most obvious Conflict in the piece occurs when my fellow passenger misses his station and I have to decide whether to drive him back or not. That may seem like a very small Conflict—and, hey, there's nothing wrong with very small Conflicts—but it actually sets off a deeper Conflict that must be resolved. What is that deeper Conflict? It's the issue of doing what is good for yours truly versus doing what is good for someone else. So it becomes a story about ethics—about the need to "always do the right thing"—and that is the value that is overtly passed on to my son in the story. In that sense, we can see that the piece fits securely into a continuum of ethical wills that we can trace back to the Bible.

Let's think about another story. How about Anne's, about singing in the choir? There the Conflict is about having difficulty producing certain sounds, tracing that difficulty to pulmonary issues, tracing those pulmonary issues to an earlier smoking habit, and feeling the guilt and shame that comes with having done something in your life that is very bad for you. That's a real and recognizable Conflict (substitute alcohol/drugs/food/sex/gambling or you name it for the very bad thing). The resolution of the Conflict is quite beautiful, however, as Anne goes beyond guilt and shame to her innate love of life and self-acceptance, expressed by making beautiful music alongside people she cares about.

So, as you can see, it helps to be able to identify Conflict so that you know what you're writing about and can engage your readers, all of whom relish Conflict and all of whom want to see how Conflict can be resolved.

Mostly when I work with writers, the challenge in finding out what the story is about is resolved by digging more deeply. Such was the case with Anne. She originally wrote her story without integrating the issue of her pulmonary problems and their source. When she dug deeper and was able to make those connections, she came away with a layered essay. That kind of layering can create a texture that you might think would be impossible to achieve in the small allotment of words you've been given.

WHAT'S THE POINT?

There are other ways for first drafts to go wrong. Let's imagine that you've written your piece and have successfully identified some recognizable Conflict. By the time you get to the end of your narrative, however, something appears to be missing. This is the time to maybe check The Point to see if it has a pulse.

It's important to differentiate between The Conflict and The Point. Your essay might be loaded with Conflict. You might, for instance, be writing about the time you were mugged and your watch, laptop, and bracelet were stolen. That's traumatic, to be sure, but bad things happen to everyone, whether that means muggings, pneumonia, getting fired, or what have you. It's not enough to merely give an account of a bad thing that has happened to you. What we do with those Conflict-ridden incidents—how we resolve them—is The Point. Putting that incident into some kind of context is crucial. For instance, I grew up in a wildly overprotective family. If I had been mugged, such an incident would push certain buttons for me, given my family history, and my "last say" might be about navigating such an event without succumbing to the feeling that the world is a minefield. That would be a perfectly good Point. And The Point doesn't necessarily have to lead you to a positive place. You might come to an older-but-wiser sort of state, let's say—or some mental state that is quite ambivalent. Again, I want to stress that The Point of a story does not have to be so neatly packaged. Rather, The Point is there to signify one all-important thing: the story's "reason to be." Why did you, the writer, want to tell this story? What should the reader take away from it? What is its justification for having been told?

The Point is an especially pressing issue for my 17-year-olds, who are competing for the attention of the time-pressed college admissions counselor and who cannot afford to leave that reader scratching his or her head. It's equally pressing, however, for the older writer who is attempting to write his or her "last say": to leave your reader or listener fruitlessly pondering your story's Point would hardly make for a fitting valedictory.

STRUCTURE AND FLOW

Let's imagine that your first draft has come in way too long (we're aiming, after all, for somewhere between 500 and 1,000 words). It is also all over the place, with digressions aplenty. Now, you're not the sort to linger in a fool's paradise. You're essentially honest with yourself. You sat down to write something very important, intending to make it really good, but it's just not working. So what went wrong?

Your Conflict and The Point seem to be in place, but perhaps the problem is that you just haven't told the story very well. Perhaps your narrative is full of extraneous details that get in the way of the reading experience. Surely you've heard the expression, "Can't see the forest for the trees." In the case of your narrative, perhaps you, and your reader, can't see the story for all the details you've piled on. The merit of your story can only really emerge when your *structure* is carefully examined and the flow is corrected as necessary.

Now is the time to recall those people in your life who are good storytellers and those who are not. You know who they are. You remember how we talked earlier in the book about those two coworkers, Mike and Phil? Phil was telling you about his dog, Ollie, and the pit bull they encountered in the dog park . . . and his ability to turn a story about an encounter with a pit bull into a complete snooze was something of a marvel, wasn't it? Mike, on the other hand, is the Irish American whose story of a fight between two soccer moms had you on the edge of your seat and in the palm of his hand. Mike had structure and flow; Phil lacked both.

How will you know whether your piece has structure

and flow and whether your incidents and details are well chosen? One way is to have others read your writing. They may be able to point out what should stay and what should go. But you, too, should be able to get a feeling for the kind of pruning that needs to be done. Chances are you'll find yourself a bit bored or distracted when you're reading the extraneous details you've included in your narrative, and you'll know it's time to "kill your babies" in order to improve flow.

In examining your structure, you may decide that you've spent too much time setting things up in the beginning and are therefore left with too little time to wrap things up at the end, and so you feel like you're playing catch-up . . . but never quite catching up. Or perhaps your middle is big and bloated and needs to go on a starvation diet. The good news is that such problems can usually be fixed, and as you move from draft to draft you'll become more attuned to these issues and will better understand how to fix them.

You might even remind yourself of how form works in writing altogether. Think of a piece of writing that is especially form-driven—a three-act play, for instance (or a screenplay, which might even be said to embrace the three-act form more closely these days than plays do). The first act, which is sometimes referred to as the "setup," introduces the characters, the situation, the location, and so on. The second act extends the situation—or the problem—

introduced in the first act. The protagonist and the antagonist do battle—physically, cerebrally, metaphorically, comically, whatever—in what is sometimes referred to as the "confrontation." In the third act, which you might think of as the "resolution," all of the loose ends are tied up and the problem is resolved. Most times, good triumphs over evil, but not always (think of the film *Chinatown*, for instance—one of the greatest screenplays of all time).

Is your "last say" going to follow this kind of form? Certainly, it does not have to do so slavishly, but the point is that form will inevitably be involved and, yes, maybe it will look like some version of the above. In the beginning, maybe you will "set up" the story, and as you tell it you will come to some kind of "confrontation" (you against someone else, you against society, you against nature, you against the frailties of your own body, whatever) and then you will "resolve" it. Thinking in terms of such a prescribed form can be very helpful as you grapple with your second draft. It's a kind of road map, and once you get your bearings, you can wander down any scenic byways you choose—*as long as you don't lose your way.*

One structure that has been effective for many of the writers I have worked with is the one I call the "sandwich" (it's actually a kind of triple-decker sandwich). In this structure, you take two actions—a here-and-now "active" action (skiing, running, knitting, drawing, gardening) and an internal action (like reflecting or reminiscing)—and you "sandwich" them together. A writer might start out in the first paragraph knitting away on a scarf—*knit one, purl two*—and in the second paragraph she'll pull back to reminisce about how she learned to knit from her grandmother. In the third paragraph it's back to the action at hand (the knitting), and in the fourth paragraph the writer goes internal again, reflecting on other things she learned from her grandmother (independence, self-reliance, ethics, whatever). In the fifth paragraph, she holds up the scarf and considers her work.

That's a very simple version of what I'm talking about—though simple can certainly be good. And a good thing almost invariably emerges from this kind of structure: you get a present action that acts as a framework upon which to hang the reflective material. If your essay was to have too much "internal action"—a surfeit of reflective material that lacks framework—it could feel full of air. In fact, the experience of reading essays that are all reflection can sometimes recall the experience of listening to someone telling you his dreams. The details might, by themselves, be interesting enough, but the overwhelming feeling is, *It's your dream. Why should I care?* The "sandwich" approach goes a long way toward mitigating that feeling. As I said, the narrative action can be quite simple (think back to Anne, who used singing in a choir as a simple narrative action), but the feeling of narrative action goes a long way toward satisfying the reader's hunger for something more substantial.

After all, most people like to read about concrete actions. They learn something new or they identify with what's being described, and that creates a connection. In the "last say" that is coming right up, you'll see how one of our writers used this technique.

RADICAL SURGERY

In terms of the big-picture editing you may be looking at in the second-draft stage, one important strategy available to you is what I call "radical surgery." This can involve lopping off whole portions of your first draft, freeing you up to move more purposefully toward a focused depiction of a smaller piece of time. That kind of surgery is often necessary, for while some writers may be capable of working with broader themes even in a space as limited as 500 to 1,000 words, most are not. Five hundred to 1,000 words is really a very small piece of real estate upon which to erect a grand edifice, and chances are that you'll find it much easier to build a trim, sturdy cabin on such a small plot of land. But don't worry—a trim, sturdy cabin can have a beauty all its own.

Mental acuity helps with this task, and, please—I don't want to hear that we baby boomers are getting too old for mental acuity. We certainly are not. At my age, I can still juggle the needs and demands of 50 students at a time and their anxious parents, and I do it all with my desktop stickies. So, in the case of your "last say," you just have to sign on to the idea of writing as a discipline and commit to the work. The work at hand is to focus—and then focus some more—and then focus some more. That may feel hard in this situation because you're thinking of this piece of writing as a kind of testament to your life and even, perhaps, a kind of valedictory, and so you want to make sure that all of the things you value about yourself and that you want people to know about you and from you will somehow emerge. Well, they won't. Not all of them. You're just creating a snapshot. But a snapshot can also be a stunning photograph, a beautiful image that will be engraved on the minds of those who witness it.

When you're thinking about where and how to reduce your chubby first draft, there's usually no better place to begin than at the beginning. In our chapter on the first draft, we touched on the topic of beginnings, and I'd just like to go back to that for a moment. As I said, beginnings can be excruciatingly tough and your problem in your second draft may still have to do with getting out of the gate.

Keep in mind that entering a piece of writing can be equally difficult for both writer and reader. In fact, entering a piece of writing—for writer and reader—is not unlike entering a body of water. It can be a lovely warm bath, an icy dip into an Alpine pool, a rush down the rapids, or any combination thereof. In any event, you, as the writer, have to take the plunge—and you have to create an environment that convinces the reader to take the plunge along with you. Sometimes I'm shocked by how stiff and clumsy my first sentences can be. "How dare you think of yourself as a writer," I might say to myself. But then, as I continue the work, a certain rhythm comes into play, the awkwardness and stiffness starts to give way, and the water? Mmmh, good.

I find that a lot of the writers I work with have a habit of beginning their pieces by telling me what they're going to say—along the lines of the openings below:

- What happened to me last summer was a revelation.
- I never felt as disappointed as I did at my daughter's wedding.
- My concept of marriage changed when I had my heart attack.

All of these sentences suggest writers who are rolling up their sleeves, and I often advise such writers to lop off those lines in which they're telling me what they're going to say and just start the story—because the fact is that there is no room for a prologue in an essay of some 500 to 1,000 words. Down the line, you may wish to write longer pieces, and that may all be well and good, but for now we are focusing on these shorter pieces because they are more manageable both for you, the writer, and for the potential orator who could be delivering your "last say" at some future point. And so, in essays of this length, you only have enough time to get into the story, tell it, and get out of it. And to show your hand as those lines above do, conveying The Point at the beginning, is really not good form.

Why don't we think back to those "last says" you've already seen in this book, and let us consider the first lines of each one?

This is the opening line of the "last say" that I wrote:

> There I stood, on the Main Concourse of Grand Central Terminal, at the information booth, as planned, holding a bag of hot pretzels from Zaro's, looking around in every direction.

With that opening line, my intention was to immerse the reader into the kind of train station experience that most of us are familiar with. "There I stood on the Main Concourse" felt different to me—and perhaps to you—than "I stood on the Main Concourse." I thought that the opening, as I wrote it, would bring the reader closer to that place and that moment, allowing for more engagement. The reader doesn't really know what's happening yet but can gather that there is some kind of plan, that I am waiting for someone, and that I have bought a bag of pretzels.

The fact that I'm not eating the pretzels myself suggests that I might have bought them for someone else. What you have here is the conveyance of information at the same time that I'm withholding information. After all, I could have started the story simply by saying, "I stood on the Main Concourse of Grand Central Terminal, waiting at the information booth for my son." But that would have been a ball with no English on it, and such dull expository sentences, particularly at the opening, barely register on a reader.

Anne, who wrote about singing in a choir, found a good way to open up her essay:

> I shape my lips into a round, "aw"-shaped smile and inhale deeply.

Initially, her piece didn't start out that way. In her first draft, the opening read like this:

> The small New England church is already full as we take our places at the front. It's deep winter, and the nine of us are swathed in sweaters and scarves—and close-fitting hats in solidarity with Laurel, our soprano soloist, a recent cancer survivor. We're all in various stages of middle age, and we're all busy; but not even the snow could keep us from singing with this committed little group.

Now that's not a bad opening, but it's a lot of information at the top of the piece. The opening she wound up using instead—shaping the lips into a round "aw"-shaped smile—manages to intrigue us, doesn't it? We wonder what's going on. Is the storyteller swimming? Is she meditating? Let's find out, we think to ourselves, immediately engaged.

Alice, the music teacher who wrote about a visit with a former student, as well as the memory of Leonard Bernstein and the "gift" that goes back and forth between teachers and students, chose to start her piece with a very straightforward opening:

> I was in my music classroom late one fall afternoon after the children had been dismissed.

There's absolutely nothing wrong with a straightforward opening (as compared to an opening that may seem straightforward—for example, "I never felt as disappointed as I did at my daughter's wedding"—but that actually spills the beans and shows your hand). In general, readers (or listeners) will not hold simple, straightforward writing against you. It's the complicated, gnarly, tangled stuff that really rubs them the wrong way. Of course, I wouldn't want to clip your wings, and if you feel you're up to writing an opening that has a bit more pizzazz, try it. Now let's see how Steve, who wrote about his mother teaching him to dance, started off his essay:

Right-left-one-two-three.

My hand, raised high, signals to start by bringing our right foot back. I'm leading a dance class to the tune of Alan Dale's famous 1955 cha-cha, "Sweet and Gentle."

An essay about dance pretty much demands some pizzazz in the delivery, and Steve recognized that and rose to the challenge. He used the first line to capture the *experience* of music—rhythm, beat, all those nice things—and that was effective.

The pieces cited above all had good beginnings, but, believe me, they didn't just happen. These writers worked at their beginnings, molding them, refining them, and sometimes starting all over again. That's the business of writing, but when you have a beginning that works—whether it's Herman Melville's *Call me Ishmael* or Steve's *Right-left-one-two-three*—it's gold.

And if you think beginnings are hard, try endings.

HOW DO I END THIS THING?

As I've said, a common problem with beginnings is that a writer will slowly take his or her time getting into the story. For the most part, I find that the opposite problem takes place around endings, when many writers virtually bail out of their pieces like parachutists jumping out of a crashing plane. In a rush to be done with the thing, highly bombastic endings like this one will sometimes rush in:

I learned my lesson on that fateful day.

Really. Truly. I did. (I can almost hear that writer saying.)

On the other hand, some endings sound like they belong to those parachutists who didn't get the parachute open in time and so, as they sink into the ocean, we get a . . . slow . . . and . . . rather pathetic . . . fade:

It's safe to say that this was a day that was really kind of memorable.

A lot of qualifiers—*really, kind of, sort of*—are dead give-aways that the writer has no idea what she or he is doing. And then sometimes I'll see an ending like this:

When I tell people this really happened, they usually don't believe me. Sometimes I'm not sure I even believe it.

That quasi-apologetic way of wrapping things up never really works. Remember that readers don't like writers who apologize. They like a writer to be in command.

Just as we've looked at the beginnings of our various "last says," why don't we have a look to see how they end? Let's start with mine:

> "You must always, always do the good thing," I said.
>   And that was enough. With a sideways glance, I saw him thinking about it. Then he put on a CD and for the rest of the trip home we listened to Dylan.

Hopefully, you are remembering my piece about meeting my son at Grand Central Terminal and teaching him something important on the ride home. Here, I state the lesson that is derived from helping the art professor who missed his station—"You must always, always do the good thing," I said—but to leave off right there would have made for a preachy ending, a kind of Aesop's Fables moral that turns choice bits of wisdom into didactic truisms. Instead, I decided to impart the wisdom but then end the piece with something more quiet and smoky, so as to let the wisdom settle in.

The next writer, Anne, who told us the story that touched on her choir, her own breathing problems, and the joy she found in singing, ended her piece this way:

> Then Laurel begins the next verse an octave above, so clear and full of feeling. It's working, for both of us, for today at least. We're breathing, and singing.
>   Aaaahhhh.

If you recall, her piece started with a "round, 'aw'-shaped smile," so that last "Aaaahhhh" finishes off her piece with a good association.

The next piece, by the music teacher Alice, concludes with a relatively straightforward ending. (Her beginning was straightforward, too—"I was in my music classroom late one fall afternoon after the children had been dismissed"—but then again Alice is a pretty straightforward kind of person.) She ends her piece this way:

> As I remembered Bernstein for what he had taught me, one of my students remembered what I taught him. I was glad that I stayed late at school that day.

I find this a graceful ending because it clearly states The Point of the essay and then somewhat tempers the directness with that quiet last sentence.

Now let's have a look at Steve's ending. Steve wrote about learning how to dance from his mother. (Isn't it interesting how many of these essays reference music?) For his ending, Steve related that early memory of dancing with his mom in the Catskills bungalow colony to his present-day situation, wherein dance serves as a tonic both for him and for others:

> In these last years when I, too, have sometimes felt a lack of gusto—exhausted with the weight of working

in fundraising and living with my wife's illness—I, like my mother, find escape and meaning in the joy of physical movement, especially dance. I reflect on the importance of having a pastime that both enriches and balances, and have come to realize that sometimes it is only later in life that we recognize some treasure of learning that we received from our parents. Meanwhile, I glance back over my shoulder and see that my Gilda ladies are smiling, sweetly and gently, as they follow my steps.

I find that to be a very rich, reflective ending to a well-worked essay. It tells me a lot about how this writer copes with what life has dealt him.

One way to come to the right ending for your piece is to understand The Point of your narrative (i.e., what drew you to this material in the first place and where your thinking about it has led you). Knowing that will help you clarify where you want to leave your readers so that they can understand The Point as well.

Beginnings and endings can be so difficult to get just right, so how can you know when you've succeeded? Probably the best indicator will be the responses of your readers. If they seem to be scratching their heads with a "Huh?" after reading your piece, then you know you have a problem and that your ending might be the culprit. Don't despair—just keep working at it. Eventually, a feeling of proportion and rhythm will enter the writing and all will be good. In other words, it will be right when it feels right. And when you read your writing aloud, as I counsel you to do, keep in mind the words of the great American composer and musician Duke Ellington, who famously said, "If it sounds good, it is good."

SHAKE UP THE STRUCTURE

With a short piece of writing, such as you're undertaking, it may not be in your best interest to tell your story in a straight, linear way. Not only does that generally take up more time than you have at your disposal, but, generally speaking, it probably doesn't engage readers as much as a narrative that plays with time. So by no means should you feel that you have to "begin at the beginning." You might begin midway through your narrative arc—or even at the end, working backward.

Keep in mind that your tone may change as you play with time. For instance, check out what happens if you start your essay with the ending. Does your essay take on more of a reflective tone? As you work your way backward, do you see the events that make up the narrative emerging as pieces of a puzzle? By playing with time, you're turning time into a player in your story.

Another interesting way to play with time is to tell

your story in *real time*. When you construct a narrative, you'll be making a number of quick cuts as you move from paragraph to paragraph, such as a filmmaker might make:

- Then we left the car park.
- I cried when we parted.
- I spent the rest of the day looking into a martini glass.

You're making these cuts because you obviously can't tell the reader everything that occurred in between—like how you ate your macaroni and cheese, watched an episode of *Breaking Bad*, and took a shower. And your reader is vastly appreciative that you have spared her those details.

Sometimes, however, you may find yourself telling a story in which you are leaving very little out—almost nothing, in fact—because you are telling (or trying to tell) your story in *real time*. This is not an easy thing to do—but if you can pull it off, it can be incredibly effective, with the reader hanging on to the edge of his or her seat. As you might imagine, this technique lends itself to the retelling of events that are: (a) short in duration and (b) intrinsically exciting. Telling the story of a board meeting, for instance, in real time would be an exquisite form of torture, even if some high-level corporate intrigue were taking place.

So then, if you're interested in telling a story about the first time you went skydiving, you could try telling that in real time. I just Googled around to find out how long a typical skydive lasts, and found out that to drop 10,500 feet takes about 70 seconds of freefall and about 5 to 6 minutes of parachuting. I then looked at www.speechinminutes.com, which has a speech calculator into which you can plug in the number of words you are planning to deliver and get the average time it takes to deliver such words in a speech. I plugged in 800 words and found out that it takes approximately 6.2 minutes to deliver that many words. So, you can see that you've got a pretty good matchup between the activity you seek to depict (skydiving), the number of words you have to work with (800), and the amount of time it might take someone to deliver your "last say" (6.2 minutes). That means that you have to get right out of that plane—no hesitation—and then you've got about 60 words in which to be absolutely terrified (or exhilarated) as you freefall and then another 700+ words to do some reflection as you're floating down in the parachute (terrified, exhilarated, or some combination) and come in for a landing. When you tell a story like that in real time, you're taking your reader (or listener) moment by moment through that experience, and that can become something quite memorable.

Those are just a couple of ways that you can play with time and, Lord knows, there are a lot more (try reading someone like Italo Calvino or Orhan Pamuk and you'll see). Indeed, playing with time is one of the best ways to "play" with writing—and when you play with writing, you and hopefully your reader may find some real joy in the bargain. And isn't joy a nice note on which to end this piece that is so much about reflecting on who you are and what you have been in the world?

The Last Say: Lydia

When I had the privilege of working with Lydia on her "last say," she was approaching 70—a very young 70. An extremely vital, dynamic person with equally strong connections to show business and the Jewish professional world, Lydia has superb taste and a fabulous home. It is a real treat to have dinner at Lydia's, not just because she's a terrific cook but also because she has a great sensibility for setting a bountiful table, often with produce from her own garden. She comes by this naturally, having grown up in South Philly in a family of Italian greengrocers, and, even though she converted to Judaism and is outstandingly erudite in all things Jewish, the piece of her that is Italian beats on as strong as ever.

When Lydia started working with me on this assignment, she opted not to go through the exploratory phase in search of a topic, as all my other writers did, but, rather, she set her mind to finishing a piece she had already started but that wasn't going anywhere. She needed to refine this piece, and the opportunity to write her "last say" gave her the impetus to go back to it. It soon became apparent, however, that her piece had altogether too many moving parts to make sense as a "last say." So she decided to take what she had done, reshape it, and scale it down for the 500- to 1,000-word limit that was the aim of this assignment.

With gustatory relish featuring strongly in her DNA, it came as no surprise that she wanted her "last say" to have something to do with food. And I immediately realized that the "sandwich" approach would make great sense for a foodie such as Lydia. If you think back to the chapter you just read, the "sandwich" approach involves taking a relatively simple narrative action and bringing along that action in short, intermittent paragraphs that are "sandwiched" with paragraphs that are reflective in nature. Knitting was the example I mentioned in the last chapter, but I've also had people write about running, swimming, dancing, playing the mandolin, and so much more. Essentially, any narrative action that doesn't require a lot of words to describe it will lend itself to this structure.

Let's have a look at Lydia's piece and see how the "sandwich" worked out for her:

Cut potatoes into small-ish cubes. Cut onions into pieces. Cut zucchini into chunks.

Oh, those zucchini! I spotted them on my pre-work morning foray to the weekly farmers' market in my

Manhattan neighborhood. From some deep recess in my mind came the image of "squash–with-the-egg-and-cheese," a dish I hadn't eaten, or even thought of, for years.

Heat olive oil in a pot. Add the cut-up vegetables. Stir constantly so they don't stick.

"Squash-with-the-egg-and-cheese" is a dish so specific to my father's Apulian family that I've never seen it anywhere else. My grandparents transported it from Faeto, their small Italian village, to South Philadelphia, where they sold fruits and vegetables in the Italian curb market above which they lived. Their six children all worked with them and, when they made families of their own, they continued to live within 10 blocks of the store and my grandparents' kitchen. Every person in the family—male, female, young, old—cooked. My grandmother taught all her grandchildren to roll gnocchi, five at a time—one for each finger. My grandfather would enter with ingredients for his pasta dishes—big wicker baskets of snails he had captured in the garden, wild mushrooms he had foraged, dandelions he had dug from sidewalk cracks. From their battered pots came the earthiest, tastiest surprises. That kitchen became the radiant center of my childhood universe.

Cook until almost tender.

South Philly was an ethnic, blue-collar neighborhood where people stayed put, and adult women wore

black for much of their life. Not the chic black hanging
in my Manhattan closet, but the black of the Southern
Italian village, worn for a year to mourn the depar-
ture of someone closely related to them, and then continuing to be worn as, inevitably, other close relatives
would die. The world of these women was the family
and the home. They were praised not for their looks,
their chic, or their accomplishments in the larger
world, but for keeping a clean, well-organized house,
rearing well-mannered children, and preparing delicious, bountiful meals. Most of my contemporaries
graduated from high school and held secretarial jobs
until they got married—usually to a boy from the
neighborhood. A very few lived at home, went to local
colleges, and became teachers.

*Puree a can of plum tomatoes in the food processor. Add
the tomatoes to the zucchini mixture. Add salt and pepper.*

I chose a different path and did the unthinkable:
I left home. The first person in my family, male or
female, to go to college, I went away for school and
then moved to New York City to live and work among
strangers. I made the life I had always dreamed of having when I was a child in South Philly, and I thrived in
this larger world of theatre, museums, friends from
around the world. Drawn to Judaism since my adoles-
cence, I fell in love with a Jewish man and converted.
My Italian family and his Russian-Jewish family

found common ground in the fact that their children had made such good choices in marrying a spouse who came from "such nice people." Our wedding took place under a *chuppah* in a friend's Manhattan apartment, and a remarkably good time was had by all.

Scramble eggs. Add grated Parmesan cheese. Turn up the heat and stir the egg and cheese into the zucchini mixture. Cook a bit more.

I tear some basil, stir it into the mixture, and let it sit for a couple of minutes. Breathing in deeply, I let the aroma fill me. Then I ladle some squash with the egg and cheese into a bowl, take a spoon from the *milchig* drawer, and sit down with it at the kitchen table. I put a spoonful in my mouth. I close my eyes.

It is just as I remembered it.

As you can see, cooking turns out to be a great action to depict in a "sandwich" essay because it really doesn't require much verbiage to move along the steps of a recipe. Also, for most people, there are few things in the world as sensual and evocative as food, and so writing about food ensures a pretty receptive audience from the get-go.

With this piece, Lydia was able to revisit her roots, exploring where she had come from and where she had gone to. It's a powerful piece—a great example of how a real narrative feeling can emerge out of some very subtle action and a great example of the "last say" as life review.

CHAPTER 6

The Third Draft

Most students I work with, whether they are teenagers or baby boomers, typically finish their pieces in about three drafts. Now, keep in mind that they are working with me, so I help them find a tight structure right at the top, which makes a major difference in terms of the number of drafts required. In any case, by the time you get to your third draft, hopefully you will have left behind any major structural issues. If all has gone as planned, you will have constructed a well-rigged ship that is ready to set sail. On the other hand, if you have built a lopsided dinghy that doesn't seem like it would make it across a pond, then this might not be the best time to focus in on the customized upholstery for your "yacht." That will be sad, but it is best to face reality and either bail out of your boat or bring it into dry dock for some major repair.

For the purposes of this chapter, let's assume that the structure of your piece is working and all of the elements are where they should be. You have constructed your piece on a solid base of Conflict, the proportions of your essay make sense, and The Point is recognizable. If you can honestly say *Check* to all that, then you can start focusing in on issues of style.

I GOT RHYTHM

As we've noted, once you enter the third-draft stage, the assumption is that your piece has developed some nice lines. The beginning, middle, and end should all bear a sound proportional relationship to one another. Your beginning is neither too short nor too long, you're not playing catch-up at the end, and you don't have a saggy midriff (well, at our age . . .). Overall, your piece has begun to develop a pleasing sense of rhythm that makes it enjoyable to read. As one of our very best writers, Elmore Leonard, once said, "I'm very much aware in the writing of dialogue, or even in the narrative, too, of a rhythm. There has to be a rhythm with it."

Pick a quiet spot and listen to your words. Does your piece have rhythm? You should be able to answer that question—and determine whether or not you have achieved the kind of flow you're aiming for. And while this may seem obvious, let's note, too, that different rhythms convey different moods. Something staccato will convey action, tension, and anxiety, whereas pieces that are characterized by more complex sentences will naturally confer more of a feeling of depth, ambiguity, reflection, and so on. It is also important to note that your rhythm—or should we say the rhythm of the reader?—can be seriously thrown off by the misplacement of punctuation. A comma in the wrong place can bring the rhythm to a momentary standstill, while a period in the wrong place can. [bring the rhythm to a crashing halt—see what I mean?]

Another thing that I am particularly allergic to and which, to my ear at least, seriously compromises the rhythm of a piece is the repetition of words from one sentence to the other. When you repeat a word from one sentence to the next, that repetition often feels tiresome, and this will not ingratiate you with your reader. So avoid repetition if you can (and have you noticed how many times I've repeated the word *repetition* in just three sentences? Case in point).

When you write a piece that is meant to be read, you are entering into a kind of contract with your reader. Implicit is the understanding that you will do whatever you can to bring certain core elements to your work, such as discipline and creativity and emotional involvement. Without such elements, you cannot hope to produce a work that will genuinely engage your reader. Therefore, the reader is not going to appreciate the dull repetition of words, because it will seem as if you had not bothered to put in the effort to find other words that would prevent that feeling of dullness. It will feel as if you simply took the easy way out.

HEARING YOUR TONE

While you're reading your piece for rhythm, listen for tone as well. Tone is an issue that many writers struggle with. When I work as an editor, I encounter a range of tones that goes from the sententious to the silly, the giddy to the glum, the ebullient to the enervated—sometimes even in the same piece.

Why do such lapses of tone occur? Often because the writer really doesn't know what he or she wants to say. In other words, in many instances, the lapses in tone are connected to a failure to understand The Point. If you don't know why you're writing something, and are simply proceeding based on the impulse to write (wherever that impulse may be coming from), then you may find yourself wandering down paths that don't necessarily hold together. If you feel that your piece is somehow inert, then maybe you're reacting by throwing in a few jokes here and there. That may be a good strategy if you're invited onto Comedy Central, but it may not be a good solution if you're attempting to capture something real and honest about your life (unless, perhaps, joke telling happens to be one of your most recognized characteristics).

If you read your piece out loud and pick up on the fact that your tone is all over the place, then the next best thing to do is to think about what your *authentic voice* is actually like. Every one of us has an authentic voice. When you're thinking about identifying marks—thumbprint, scars, dental work—your authentic voice should be thrown into the mix. Some of us are warm, some wry; some down to earth, some imperious; some pious, some profane. Now, as a writer of fiction, you can put your authentic voice aside and assume an entirely different voice. I once wrote an entire novel in the voice of a woman who lived in a small town and worked as a receptionist in a dentist's office. It was a great writing experience for me because half the fun of writing fiction is doing just that: throwing off your authentic voice and trying to simulate the authentic voice of someone else. Given that this is your "last say," however, let's assume that you'll want it to be in your own authentic voice so as not to play any tricks on your loved ones (unless, of course, you're a noted practical joker and it makes great sense for you to do just what I suggested you wouldn't want to do).

Take a moment to reflect on how you think people hear you. I know the way most people would describe my authentic voice—some combination of warm, ironic, sarcastic, articulate, humorous—but how do you think you are generally heard? Consider some of the words below and think if any of them apply to you:

- Argumentative
- Audacious
- Authoritative
- Bland
- Blunt
- Calm
- Caustic
- Cheerful
- Cynical
- Detached
- Dour
- Dramatic
- Enthusiastic
- Flippant
- Intense
- Laconic
- Melancholy
- Pedantic
- Phlegmatic
- Sweet
- Sympathetic

- Vibrant
- Whimsical
- Wistful

This can be an interesting exercise—something you may never have thought about before. And some of it can be a bit . . . shall we say, uncomfortable? "Pedantic"? You're not so fast to sign up for that one, I'm sure, but be honest with yourself. Has anyone ever compared you to Cliff Clavin, the mail carrier on *Cheers*? Then, I'm afraid, you may legitimately qualify as pedantic.

"Laconic," you say? Well, have you ever been termed a "strong, silent type"? Ever been compared to Gary Cooper or Clint Eastwood? Then own up to that laconic nature, be proud of it, and reflect it in your "last say." Of course, it's likely that you will do that naturally and write far more the way one might imagine Clint Eastwood writing than the way Richard Simmons writes (does Richard Simmons write?), but the desperation that develops around a piece of writing when things just aren't going the way they should can lead a writer into strange places and suddenly that Richard Simmons voice is present and you honestly don't know why.

While it is interesting to play with the diagnostic above and try to determine whether your authentic voice is "wistful" or "audacious," perhaps a better way to begin is to think about whether your authentic voice leans more to the formal or the informal. I know, for instance, that I have quite an informal nature. One of the first things I always tell my 17-year-old students when we start to work together is for them to call me "Alan." (Most do, but some cannot get beyond the "respect" of calling me Mr. Gelb, even though I don't believe that respect emanates from titles.) I know other people my age who couldn't imagine not being called Mr. or Mrs., and that doesn't speak ill of them. That's just their nature.

In this assignment, however, you may want to veer a bit from your base position, whether that's formal or informal, and head more to the middle. In other words, in terms of informal versus formal prose, let the informal among us apply a little more rigor to our authentic voices and steer away, for once, from the very breezy, chatty tone that can quickly start to sound like a not-very-well-written young adult novel. (*Seriously, everybody, when I say that I was confused, I'm not kidding. I was absolutely out of my gourd.*) That tone can quickly cloy, and your audience, stuck in their seats at a memorial service, may soon be wearing empty grins. By the same token, the stuffy, pompous, formal, John Kerry-esque tone that I sometimes see can be equally egregious. (*Let it be said that confusion prevailed, and my powers of acuity failed me in the extreme.*) When that tone sets in, your audience will start to look at their watches, covertly check e-mail, play Angry Birds, or just drift off to sleep. So, unless you're a genuine stylist who can carry off a tone that is squarely on one side of this aisle or another, you'll probably want to aim for something in the middle. That doesn't mean that you're going to be writing prose that feels impersonal or even generic. Hardly. Instead, you're going to use good writing—which, for most people, means strong muscular prose that is uncluttered and clean—to get across aspects of your authentic voice that really matter, allowing them to come through in a way that might get lost within a tone that is overly formal or informal.

It's also interesting to note that an overly formal tone can enter your writing not because you're an especially formal person but, rather, because your insecurity about writing is pushing you into a place where your awkward, stiff constructions are making you come across as more formal than you actually are. Many people equate "good" writing with "formal" writing, particularly those of us baby boomers who were taught to write in a certain way. Some of us still approach an important writing assignment, like this "last say," as if we were invited to a *très* posh dinner and were worried about which fork to use for the shrimp cocktail. We allow ourselves to get so immersed in the rules of writing that we forget the most important "rule" of all: find and use your authentic voice.

A lack of good, clean, muscular sentence structure can result in that stiff, formal feeling in other ways as well. For instance, I often see constructions that use the phrase *to be* in ways that are decidedly clunky:

- I found *Cold Mountain* to be a very moving book.
- I would like there to be more of a connection between me and my sister.
- In order to retire, there would need to be a much
  better plan in place.

As sentences go, none of the above is a prizewinner.
How could they be rewritten in a way that would loosen
them up, save precious words, and thereby save the reader
the work of plowing through them? Consider the following
makeovers:

- *Cold Mountain* moved me greatly.
- I am hoping to connect more with my sister.
- In order to retire, I need to put a better plan in
  place.

Do you see the more active feeling in those sentences?
Do you see an increased immediacy that takes the place of
the stiffness that was there?

The passive voice will also lend a formal, stuffy tone to
your writing—even if you're not a formal, stuffy person.
I'm sure you have studied the pitfalls of the passive voice at
some other point in your life, but maybe it was, like, *40
years ago*? So let's refresh our shaky memories, if you will.

In the case of a sentence that is written with an active
voice, somebody or something performs an action. In the

case of a sentence that is written with a passive voice, the action is being done *to* somebody or something. Consider these examples:

Active: The golfer hit the ball 100 yards.
Passive: The ball was hit 100 yards by the golfer.

Active: Emily tutored a boy from the inner city.
Passive: An inner-city boy was tutored by Emily.

Active: Rudy accepted his award from the Neighborhood Association.
Passive: The Neighborhood Association award was accepted by Rudy.

If you read these sentences in their active and passive modes, it seems almost inevitable that you would prefer the active mode—which makes you wonder what kind of writer would choose the passive mode instead. The answer is *almost any kind of writer.* Thank goodness for spellchecker—one of the handy things it does is point out when we lapse into the passive voice. It's not altogether clear why people seem to fall into that voice, which feels so inanimate, but I do have a theory. I think that many of us feel deeply insecure when it comes to writing, and we unconsciously choose the passive voice because that voice reflects that insecurity (being done *to* instead of doing). Whatever the case, you'll help your cause considerably if you stay with active constructions. That's what people like to read. That said, is the passive voice ever justified? I suppose. If, for instance, you're writing a fictional piece in which you are portraying a passive character, then a passive voice might be appropriate. Otherwise, I would advise you to avoid it, which is relatively easy to do.

Just to recap, we've seen how several writing issues can lead you down the road to a formality that will win you few fans. These issues include using the passive voice and using the "to be" construction. I want to give equal time, however, to informality, too much of which can quickly degrade the level of your essay.

One way I see informality coming through in essays is in a reliance on phrases like "you know" or "seriously" or "literally" or "really":

- You know, for me, there's nothing like an ice-cold beer on a summer day.
- Seriously, I had just about had it with Max, even if he was my own son.
- We were literally stuck in traffic for four hours.
- I was really, really steamed by the time Leo met me at the restaurant.

As you may already have gathered from your reading of this book, I like a conversational tone. Most people do.

As I've mentioned, I work extensively in the area of higher education marketing, and much of what I write is for the purposes of recruitment. I write those big glossy brochures, called "viewbooks," that students and their parents schlep home from their college visits. In those pieces, I always aim for a warm, conversational tone because I know that it engages people. I don't try to sound like a 17-year-old because, at my age, to try to sound like a 17-year-old would be the absurd equivalent of wearing my baseball cap backward. So, I avoid anything that sounds like slang, which dates faster than a carton of cottage cheese anyway. I also write many pieces that can be labeled "development" pieces. (*Development* is sort of a nice word for *fundraising*). In those pieces, I generally aim at an audience that is anywhere between fortysomething and . . . end-of-life. Those kinds of pieces—and I'm sure you get plenty of them—often have a stultifying institutional tone, with ghastly words like *conceptualization* and *potentialize* and *optimize* and *impactful*. (We will return to the issue of jargon later in the book.) I try to avoid that institutional tone in my development pieces because, for the most part, rich, important people have feelings, too. So I also bring in the warm, conversational tone there when I can—at least, as much the development officers at the colleges and universities allow me to.

That said, there is definitely such a thing as being too informal. Usually, too much informality enters into a piece for the same reason as too much formality: because the writer is actively struggling with tone. He or she doesn't know how to inject a feeling of life into the piece through well-chosen incident and tight structure, so, instead, there is an overreliance on catchy words or phrases:

> Dressed up in my cutaway coat for Alison's wedding, I
> looked into the mirror and thought to myself, "You're
> a pretty spiff father of the bride, Jack."

"Spiff"? Really, Jack? (And, while we're on the subject, that phrase "Really?" as I have just used it is also getting very old already—as is the expression "getting very old.")

In short, your goal in your "last say," is to sound like you. And why should that be so hard?

The Last Say: Dan One thing that particularly strikes me when I work with adult writers is that they really do have a lot more to "review" when it comes to life review than my 17-year-olds do. That simple equation—more life = more life review—can make the exploratory process involved in finding a topic far more challenging for older folks than it is for younger ones. My friend Dan, who agreed to be part of one of my trial groups, was a case in point.

As Dan went through the exploratory process, he veered off in many directions, as most of us do. In a number of responses, however, he returned to what had probably been the central trauma of his life: the death of his mother when he was a young boy. As he explored ideas for his "last say," it seemed, for a while at least, that he might wind up writing a recollection of spreading his mother's ashes at the family retreat on Cape Cod.

Over time, however, Dan decided that he wanted to go in a different direction. He was intent on leaving something for his two daughters that would help them know their father better—a very good goal for one's "last say"—but the part of himself that he wanted to reveal was about an experience in his work life when he stood up for a principle. Knowing Dan as I did, I recognized that he was a highly principled person who saw himself very much in the world, thinking and writing about the law and politics.

In fact, Dan, who is a lawyer, had spent most of his professional life writing for a legal publication. He was well known and well thought of in that world and, now retired, he actively continued his work, blogging about the same sorts of issues he had been writing about for years.

And so, the direction that Dan went in for his "last say" made good sense for him. While it feels less internal than some of the other essays that came out of this process, I think it stands as a good example of how an essay that is less internal can still feel highly personal and come across as a piece of family history that has real meaning for those who have shared their lives with the writer.

Here is Dan's "last say":

In 2001, 18 years after I joined the *New York Law Journal* as a reporter, I was asked to sign a union card. For weeks, I dodged the request. I had had an experience with union organizing years earlier, when I was a lawyer with a program providing free legal services for the poor, and the whole thing blew up in my face. I was the one asking coworkers to sign cards and went on to become president of the union chapter, but eventually I was promoted to a low-level management position and within a matter of weeks the union went on strike. The picketers took to chanting my name, demanding that I join them (which I couldn't do without being fired). Even my then-wife, as a member of a related union, joined the picket line.

On the other hand, I was dismayed that the Supreme Court had installed George W. Bush as president, and saw the union effort at the *Law Journal* as a way of exorcising that horrible defeat for both the Democratic Party and unions. The fact is that my political DNA was as a Roosevelt reformer. My dad had been a New Deal Democrat, and my earliest political memories were of going to an Adlai Stevenson parade in 1952 and soliciting donations from neighbors in the 1956 campaign. The union effort also held the prospect of a tempting prize. The *Law Journal* was owned by American Lawyer Media (ALM), which had an empire of dozens of legal news publications across the country. Organizing ALM's 900 employees might well help reverse the Democratic Party's sagging fortunes.

My many months of temporizing came to a halt when a coworker confronted me. "Are you in or not?" she asked. I was in.

Shortly after I signed up, ALM's chief executive, Bill Pollak, summoned me to his office. I think I was the one he picked because, in Malcolm Gladwell's parlance, he saw me as the "tipping point." I was the paper's most experienced reporter and had raised the paper's public profile with controversial stories. During the union drive, the New York State Bar Association gave me an award in recognition of my reporting at the paper.

At the meeting, Pollak came right to the point. "What is your grievance?" he demanded to know. "What does the staff want?"

"I want a union," I answered—completely true, if impolitic.

Pollak then warned, "We can do this the easy way or the hard way."

True to his word, Pollak hired a high-powered law firm to fight us at every turn and the scare tactics began. Three of us, including myself, were threatened with possible termination for leaving union flyers in the advertising department; all editorial staffers (even the secretary) were required, either alone or in small groups, to attend meetings with top company officials; and a coworker warned me that Pollak had been telling staffers not to let "Dan Wise lead you around by the nose."

The tactics succeeded. We all were frightened. Without the protection of a union, we were certain our jobs would be doomed.

It became a war of attrition, but we felt we had no choice but to hang tough. After months of preliminary legal skirmishes, "negotiations" finally began. For more than a year, the only word we heard from management at the bargaining table was "no."

Finally, the union organizers said we had to either ramp up our tactics or fold our cards. They wanted us to picket a trade fair, which ALM sponsored each year at the Hilton Hotel in midtown. So on a cold January morning a group of about 15 of us formed a picket line. After an hour or so, Pollak appeared and marched right up to me. Standing well within my personal space, he shouted, "Get your people out of here."

I was frozen. I just stood mute as he berated me, afraid I was going to pee in my pants. But I stood fast.

As soon as Pollak retreated, we all realized something extraordinary had happened. We had won the war of attrition! Pollak had cracked first. His threat and demands, made in public view before all 15 of us, gave the union leverage because they appeared to violate federal labor law. In short order, the company finally made some concessions, and we had our union.

Even though Bush was reelected in 2004 and only 30 of us were covered by the union, it was worth it. We had persevered and kept each other's backs despite the company's huge financial advantages and its control over our professional lives. We had survived and prevailed. What could be sweeter than that?

This is a good story, well told, and I think that, in terms of Dan's goals, it does show a part of himself that might otherwise have gone unnoted. For me, it is so interesting to see how individuals approach this exploratory phase of the work. It's a revelation to observe their process and to watch as the writer zeroes in on a piece of himself or herself that calls out for expression. Since we are all so multifaceted, the decision that surrounds choosing that special element that you want people to know about you strikes me as profound.

So then is Dan's story a good story to read at a memorial service? Such a decision is up to the family, friends—and the writer himself. There are no set rules to any of this. In terms of Dan's essay, I hope it will be a very long time before I hear it read at a memorial service, but I guess the real answer to the question of whether or not it would work in that context is to read it out loud and see how it plays. As I quoted Duke Ellington earlier in the book, *If it sounds good, it is good.* So gather a few trusted souls around you some evening, read your "last say," and see how it goes. The good news is that such an evening should be interesting for everyone, and even if this one doesn't ring the right bells, you should know that you have many more stories within you, waiting to come out.

CHAPTER 7

Polishing

The issues that we began to talk about in Chapter 6, "The Third Draft," carry over into this next phase of the work, when the goal is to burnish our pieces as best we can. Often, when I work with writers, young and older alike, they are astonished to see the level of attention that this work demands. Every word, every comma, every every-thing is pored over. It has to be. You must understand that a misplaced comma can hold up your readers and throw them off balance, and to get them back on balance, even from such a seemingly minor infraction, is not easy to do. That momentary lapse of attention that occurs when a comma lands in the wrong place or a word is used incor-rectly or a metaphor feels stale and trite means an inter-ruption of the rhythm of the reading experience.

Therefore, in pursuit of burnished beauty, we will

devote this chapter to all of the small problems that can undermine the level of your writing. Many small problems, after all, can add up to a big problem. It pains me to see a good story sabotaged by technical difficulties—but I see that all the time. So let's get started on finding and solving these problems.

KEEP IT CLEAN

Just as some people are natural athletes or are naturally gifted at music or math, so are some people lucky enough to be natural writers. They just have a certain innate rhythm to their work that makes their writing, even when it's rough, basically pleasurable to read. Most people don't have that gift—but that doesn't mean they shouldn't write. Of course they should. Everyone should. It just means that maybe they shouldn't try to go down black-diamond slopes.

I routinely suggest to my college applicant writers that they keep their essays clean and simple. I say the same thing to my adult writers, but they tend to resent that suggestion. Well, that's not so surprising, I suppose. The kids are trying to get into good schools, so they'll listen to pretty much anything I have to say. The adults, however, are less impressionable and more proprietary when it comes to sharing their life experiences. Sometimes, however, the adults will come around and see the sense of what I am saying. And what I am saying can basically be boiled down to the one pithy thought I mentioned earlier: *a reader will never hold clean, simple writing against you.* Seriously. It's the thorny, tangled stuff that drives readers crazy, and why shouldn't it? It takes time to untangle something. Think about those long orange extension cords that we keep in our basements. Are you picturing what it's like to untangle one of those? Problem sentences are a lot like those extension cords. Someone skilled, like myself, can work out the kinks, but amateur writers left on their own too often present tangled "extension cords" to their readers, and naturally the reader resents it. No one wants to put in extra work to read something. We want it delivered to us nice and clean.

One of the best ways to achieve a reasonably good, clean standard of writing is to simply start a sentence with a noun and a verb. Now, I can't really afford in this slim book to get into a comprehensive discussion of sentence structure, but a few well-chosen points can make a big difference in how your writing turns out. I know it's been a long time since you learned about subjects and predicates (do you remember how we used to have to diagram sentences? I think that's a thing of the past), but let me just remind you that every sentence has to have one of each: one subject (at least) and one predicate (at least). The subject, which is a noun, is the thing that is doing the action, which is expressed by the predicate, a verb. *The drink* is not a sentence. Why? It has no predicate. *I drink* is a sentence, albeit a rather primitive life-form, because *I* is a subject, *drink* is a predicate, and so the minimum requirements for a sentence are met. *The drink quenches* is another simple but correct sentence. In this instance, the *drink* becomes the subject (and we could substitute, if we wished, the Coke, the tonic, the water, the Ramos gin fizz, or countless other subjects, and it would still work). *Quenches* is the predicate (but we could substitute *spills, intoxicates, satisfies,* or many other verbs).

Some of the most problematic writing I encounter could be headed off at the pass if the writers would just begin their sentences with a subject and a predicate. Those gnarly orange extension cords would then go away. Here is what one of those problem sentences sounds like:

> From this experience although I have grown dis-
> traught over atrocities in the world, I have become a
> tad bit wiser and knowledgeable of who I am and what
> I want to do on the rest of my journey called life.

This is someone who does not have the natural writing talent to pull off a sentence starting with a prepositional phrase. She's very bright, very accomplished, but does not happen to be a natural writer. That is not a fate worse than death, however, and she should be relieved to know that she is not alone. When I shared with her the helpful hint of starting a sentence with a noun and a verb (subject and predicate), her writing began to sort itself out and sentences like the above started to sound like this (with some extra editing to get rid of some of the other egregious issues, like "a tad" wiser):

> I have become wiser and more knowledgeable about who I am and what I want to do in life as a result of this experience, even though I am sometimes distraught about the atrocities in the world.

Hey. It's not a prizewinner, I realize that, but readers aren't going to resent her because of it. And the cure was simple. *I have* is a noun (I) and a verb (have) right at the beginning of the sentence, where it serves to anchor her so she does not get lost quite as easily as she usually does. So just store that away in your treasure chest of good writing tips. *If you don't want to get lost in a sentence, start with a subject and a predicate.*

Generally, when I talk about "keeping it clean," I'm talking about clearing away the clutter from your writing. Let's keep Mies van der Rohe's famous dictum in mind: *less is more.* These memorable words were a reaction, in part, to the design precepts of the Victorian, Edwardian, and French Empire eras. In those times, the sitting room ran amok with doilies on overstuffed chairs, tassels on the drapes, beaded shades on the lamp, Egyptian cat statues, Grecian-style urns, and all manner of dado, ormolu, and what have you. The design principles that followed, based on clean lines and natural textures and light, felt like a breath of fresh air. Now think about this: in writing your "last say," do you want your audience to be focused on your "beaded lamp shade" (i.e., your complicated metaphor), or do you want to make sure that the truth and the power of what you have to say come through? If it's the latter, which I suspect is the case, then stay away from the thesaurus, put aside the unnecessary adjectives and adverbs, control your metaphors, and limit your exclamation points to evoking emergency situations. Now let's look at some of those issues individually.

THE THESAURUS TRAP

We baby boomers were raised to carry our Roget's with us. Nowadays, as our memories become less reliable, there is definitely a place for the crowning achievement of Peter Mark Roget, the British physician who dedicated himself to collecting words, publishing his masterwork in 1852 as the *Thesaurus of English Words and Phrases Classified and Arranged so as to Facilitate the Expression of Ideas and Assist in Literary Composition*. In the course of my writing, I will sometimes consult a Roget's just to remind myself of some nice words out there that I might have forgotten. Almost always, however, these are words I know. Having an excellent vocabulary is a great boon for a writer because the meaning of a word is generally precise. Now if I were to decide that *precise* was just a humdrum word and I headed in search of something a little sexier, I might go to my thesaurus and find a veritable treasure trove of words that raced my motor. Wow! Look! I can choose from *meticulous* and *punctilious* and *fastidious* and . . . Whoa! Stop the presses!

While these words are listed as synonyms, it would be pretentious and ostentatious and just plain wrong to use them in place of the word *precise* in the sentence, "Having an excellent vocabulary is a great boon for a writer because the meaning of a word is precise." If you rewrite this as ". . . because the meaning of a word is meticulous," then you will definitely be off. People can be meticulous—think Mary Poppins—but words? I don't think so. *Punctilious?* Again, it's a people word, and rather more intense than *meticulous.* Someone who pays attention to how napkins are folded could be said to be punctilious. *Fastidious* is even further along on the uptight scale. Fastidious people wouldn't be caught dead eating ribs at a barbecue. But words cannot be fastidious, so you run the risk of making yourself sound foolish if you go leafing through your thesaurus on the assumption that all synonyms are created equal. You need to understand context and connotation in order to use a word correctly. And please remember what I said earlier: *a reader will never hold clean, simple writing against you.* Most readers are very happy with good, clean prose that does not require that they have a dictionary at the ready. This may explain why Ernest Hemingway was so popular.

ANNOYING ADJECTIVES

Adjectives. Who needs 'em? As with most thesaurus-driven language, the bulk of adjectives can be left behind and a reader will thank you for it. In fact, it is a safe bet to say that there is an overlap between these two problems—thesaurus-driven language and adjectival abuse, as I'll wager that a good 90 percent of thesaurus use is connected to the hunt for adjectives. Many people feel that it is not enough to say, "Scout was a dog with a clearly established role in the home." It has to be, "Scout was a (dignified) (noble) (princely) dog with a clearly established role in the home." These writers seem to think that a noun is some-how "underdressed" if it doesn't have an adjective con-nected to it, but I personally don't want to see a lot of words connected to a dog. Generally, as a reader, I want to see character emerge through action. Let me see Scout waiting patiently for his dinner to be placed in the bowl, rather than charging at it like a warthog. That tells me something about him—dignity, nobility—that mere adjectives cannot.

Let me give you an example of a piece of text in which the adjectives are churning:

There, on the capacious stage of the Metropolitan Opera, the statuesque soprano with the titian hair and penetrating gaze let loose with some of the most mellifluous singing I had ever heard.

So then, let's see how many ways this sentence went wrong. First of all, the stage at the Metropolitan Opera is not "capacious" (thesaurus trouble again). A handbag can be capacious, but the Metropolitan Opera stage, if you felt compelled to adjective-ize it, would maybe be "huge" or "immense" or "enormous." But this is an excellent example of when an adjective is called for and when it is not. The reader naturally assumes that the stage of the Metropolitan Opera is hardly small. After all, we're not talking about the Upper Montclair Community Theatre. So, immediately, we can dispense with the need to adjective-ize that section, and here is what it now sounds like:

There, on the stage of the Metropolitan Opera, the statuesque soprano with the titian hair and penetrating gaze let loose with some of the most mellifluous singing I had ever heard.

All right then. Moving ahead, we now have the issue of "the statuesque soprano." This is a particularly egregious example of adjective-izing, as "the statuesque soprano" sounds like she comes right out of a Perry Mason mystery.

(Actual titles by Perry Mason's creator, Erle Stanley Gardner, who adored alliteration, included *The Case of the Hesitant Hostess, The Case of the Glamorous Ghost,* and *The Case of the Cautious Coquette.*) While alliteration can be a useful literary device, here, with the "statuesque soprano," it feels ridiculous. And do we even have to know that the soprano has attractive dimensions? Probably not. So let's see what it looks like now in a pared-down version:

> There, on the stage of the Metropolitan Opera, the soprano with the titian hair and penetrating gaze let loose with some of the most mellifluous singing I had ever heard.

Again, let's decide whether or not we need the physical detail of the soprano's hair color. Is that relevant to anything? Probably not, but if you decide that you must establish that the soprano is redheaded, let's just say she is. "Titian-haired" sounds like what MGM publicity flacks might have come up with for Rhonda Fleming—very 1950s—so, again, keep it simple and clean (if you must refer to her hair color):

> There, on the stage of the Metropolitan Opera, the red-headed soprano with the penetrating gaze let loose with some of the most mellifluous singing I had ever heard.

OK. Now we're up to "penetrating gaze." Ugh. It makes me think of Bela Lugosi. Of course her gaze is intense; she's trying to hit an A-flat over high C, for goodness sake. So let's leave that out altogether:

There, on the stage of the Metropolitan Opera, the redheaded soprano let loose with some of the most mellifluous singing I had ever heard.

Now you know I was going to go thumbs-down on "let loose." It sounds rather vulgar in this context. Rodeo riders let loose with whoops when they sit atop steers, but I don't like that expression for opera singers. So I'm changing it to this:

There, on the stage of the Metropolitan Opera, the redheaded soprano poured forth with some of the most mellifluous singing I had ever heard.

And that brings us to "mellifluous singing." Ugh. *Mellifluous* actually means "sweet or musical; pleasant to hear." When I spoke to the writer of this sentence, she told me that what she had wanted to convey was that the soprano hit it out of the park. So instead of the dulcet-tinged "mellifluous," we used "powerful," which everyone knows the meaning of and which means something quite different from "mellifluous." So the final version of this particular bit of text reads as follows:

> There, on the stage of the Metropolitan Opera, the soprano poured forth with some of the most powerful singing I had ever heard.

Now we can all clearly see what that moment was about, and you can also see that the "redheaded" bit fell by the wayside, too (it turned out that we didn't need to know the color of the soprano's hair, after all). Those silly adjectives—"statuesque," "titian," "penetrating," "mellifluous"—were really bringing nothing to the party and when they went away, nobody missed them. And perhaps the real reason that they were not missed is because readers—and listeners—inevitably seem to prefer text that has fewer words. Not only does it require less time to read the thing, but there's also a spare, simple grace that allows you to conjure up an image more easily than the longer version, which tries to *supply* the image.

Keep in mind that a good writer doesn't feel compelled to do the reader's work. A good writer recognizes the implicit collaboration in the writing-reading relationship, in which both parties have a role to play, and so the good writer doesn't color in every picture and explain every action, every relationship, and every nuance of the story. A good writer is respectful of the *mind's eye*—that plane of consciousness upon which readers can bring to bear their own associations and references.

To get a sense of good writers, it always makes sense to *go* to good writers. There isn't a better one, as far as I'm concerned, than Alice Munro, which may explain why she was awarded the 2013 Nobel Prize in Literature. Here is a short section from her story "Post and Beam," in which the central character is seeing her cousin for the first time in years:

> Some things about Polly's looks Lorna had forgotten. How tall she was and what a long neck and narrow waist she had, and an almost perfectly flat chest. A bumpy little chin and a wry mouth. Pale skin, light-brown hair cut short, fine as feathers. She looked both frail and hardy, like a daisy on a long stalk. She wore a ruffled denim skirt with embroidery on it.

Most of the words that make up this description are quite straightforward: "tall," "long," "narrow," "flat." Then along come a few that are more surprising: "a bumpy little chin and a wry mouth." These more surprising words bring you deeper into the experience and set you up for the similes: "fine as feathers," "like a daisy on a long stalk." And with that phrase—"a daisy on a long stalk"—the reader completes the picture, seeing the character quite vividly.

How differently this would read if it were bollixed up with "titian" hair and "mellifluous" singing.

I think it's safe to say that nowhere in the world is economy more prized than in the reading experience. (Well, maybe at Walmart on Black Friday.) Even with regard to a filmgoing experience, economy seems less an issue, as we don't necessarily mind soft-focus interludes of photogenic stars romping through fields of clover. (Picture Katharine Ross and Robert Redford on bikes to the tune of "Raindrops Keep Falling on My Head" in *Butch Cassidy and the Sundance Kid*.) In the reading experience, however, when it is just words, we, the readers, had better be convinced that those words are there for a reason. If not, there are a hundred things we'd rather do—and will do.

AGGRAVATING ADVERBS

As unwelcome as annoying adjectives may be, I think, if I had to choose, I would say that unnecessary adverbs are even more perturbing.

Now what's wrong with an adverb? you ask. Right proper part of speech, ain't it, guv?

Well, yes, there is a use for adverbs—a *limited* use. When I see a proliferation of these little critters, I generally see, at the same time, a swan dive in the level of writing. Going back to issues of right and wrong, here are some

examples of adverbs that are used in ways that are not offi-
cially wrong:

> Rhoda reacted *violently* to the touch of the spider.
> The ballerina moved *deftly* across the dance floor.
> The partygoers laughed *uproariously* at the come-
> dian.

As I say, there's nothing legally amiss about those
underlined adverbs. You're not going to get arrested for
them. On the other hand, they're not going to win you any
writing awards.

Even though you may be using adverbs within their
legal limits, in general they don't make for particularly
lively writing. You would be better off in most cases finding a nice, strong verb to take the place of those clunky
adverbial constructions. And think about it: what are those
adverbs actually telling you? When I read that Rhoda
reacted "violently" to the touch of the spider, I don't know
whether she screamed, lost bodily control, smashed it with
her open palm, or what. On the other hand, if you tell me
that Rhoda *flinched* at the touch of the spider or Rhoda
fainted at the touch of the spider or Rhoda *blanched* at the
touch of the spider, I can then conjure up useful images in
my mind that will help me with the reading experience.
Similarly, why tell me that the ballerina moved "deftly"
across the dance floor? Ballerinas are, almost by definition,

deft. That is to say, there is a very small market indeed for clumsy ballerinas. But if you tell me that the ballerina *floated* across the dance floor or *glided* across the dance floor or *leapt* across the dance floor, again I see pictures in my mind. And just so that last example won't be left behind, the partygoers who laughed "uproariously" at the comedian also tell me little. There are many words that are designed to convey different levels and modes of laughter, so why not use one of them? The partygoers *guffawed* means that they split their seams. The partygoers *tittered* means that they might have heard something naughty. The partygoers *chuckled* suggests that they were listening to a more gentle kind of comedian (but please, as a personal favor, don't use the word *chuckle* ever).

While a bad adjective just tends to hold up the writing, a bad adverb can point a piece toward absurdity. Some of you may remember from our youth the Tom Swift novels about the boy scientist. These were a formative influence on people who later became important to the field of science—people like Ray Kurzweil, Robert Heinlein, and Isaac Asimov—but they became equally important as cautionary tales of adverb abuse. Tom Swift, Boy Scientist, had the unfortunate habit of spouting "Tom Swifties." These risible constructions always included an adverb with ridiculous results. Do a Google search on Tom Swifties and you'll quickly get the idea, as you consider such head-scratchers as these:

- "Gin!" Tom said winningly, spreading out his cards.
- "Hurry up and get to the back of the ship!" Tom said sternly.
- "Careful with that chainsaw!" Tom said offhandedly.
- "Do you like hockey?" Tom asked puckishly.
- "I forgot what I was supposed to buy," Tom said listlessly.

Well, we could go on all day. And allow me to extend a blanket acknowledgment to all those anonymous wits who came up with those.

I don't tend to see that level of absurdity very much in the writing that comes my way (although sometimes I do), but I certainly do see examples of adverb abuse that clog up the page with sentences like these:

- The burglar silently retreated from the room.
- The principal cautiously sidestepped the question.
- Helen posed coquettishly in the mirror.

Once again, the quickest fix for clunky adverbial constructions is to simply find a good, solid verb to take their place. Hence, the burglar *slipped* from the room or the principal *evaded* the question or Helen *preened* in the mirror would all work well. This is where a good vocabulary comes in handy, so make a note that it's never too late to start keeping a word bank (and as we must now say pro forma to people our age these days, doing something like that opens up new neural pathways blah blah blah).

MALADROIT METAPHORS

As you scrutinize your essay at this stage, you will also want to cast your gimlet eye on your metaphors—if you have any. And trust me—there's nothing wrong with not having any. No metaphors are altogether better than bad metaphors. Also, while we're on the subject, a gimlet eye is, I suppose, a form of metaphor. For most of us, "gimlet" only refers to one thing: the lime-tinged vodka or gin drink. In fact, the expression "gimlet eye"—which means an eye that appears to give a sharp and piercing look—can be traced back originally in print to 1752 and connects to the gimlet, "a small, sharp, woodworking tool with a screw point, grooved shank, and cross handle for boring holes." Therefore, we are talking about the eye as a gimlet and therefore we are invoking a metaphor. Interesting . . . if you like that sort of thing.

Great writers use great metaphors. When you read a book by a great writer, you're almost sure to encounter gorgeous metaphors that may stay in your mind long after you've finished reading. As I've said, however, we are not all great writers—and you don't have to be a great writer to write a powerful "last say." You can simply tell your story in an honest and authentic way that engages readers without fanfare. But even those of us who are not great writers might come up with a great metaphor. It's altogether possible. So we have to have some sense of a scale by which to judge these features, going from the ridiculous to the sublime.

And there you have it—a cliché. *The ridiculous to the sublime.* What is a cliché? Generally, it is a metaphor that initially has some power, which leads it to being used over and over and over again until it becomes a whopping cliché of the sort that people rely on because it's easier than coming up with their own metaphors. So the ridiculous to the sublime is a metaphorical construction that we've all heard countless times and it tends to *go in one ear and out the other* (cliché).

A good *rule of thumb* (cliché) regarding metaphors is that if they sound as though you've heard them before, *don't use them.* The likelihood is that they're clichés. Just to make sure we're all *on the same page* (cliché), let's define a *cliché* as a terminally tired expression that *has been around the block too many times* (cliché) and is ready to be *retired to the farm* (cliché).

Is it ever appropriate to use a cliché? About the only instance I can think of is if you're using it in connection with a character. In other words, let's imagine that your "last say" is about a teacher you had early in life who spouted clichés. You've chosen to write this piece because you feel that the experience of suffering through English teacher Mr. Burrows, whose every sentence made reference to "good as gold" or "busy as a bee" or "dead as a doornail," was instrumental in motivating you to see the world in a more original way. In my mind, that would be a suitable justification for using clichés in your essay.

A phrase can actually become a cliché on *the turn of a dime* (cliché). We all hear expressions out there in the zeitgeist that we think sound cool, and we believe that, if we use them, we will seem cool and in the know. And so we *buy into them* (cliché). Before we know it, we—and our dry cleaner, our insurance agent, and our pharmacist—are *thinking outside the box, putting in the sweat equity,* and *knocking one out of the park.*

Closely connected to the issue of clichés—almost *blood brothers* (cliché)—is the issue of jargon. Jargon is the specialized or technical language of a particular profession, trade, or group of people. It can often sound excluding, smug, and self-important—and it's all over the place.

Jargon, as the definition suggests, emerges from a variety of fields. As a result, the everyday speech of the populace (that is, you and me) is filled with expressions that come from show business, the sports arena, the business world, the military, the political arena, the legal profession, and more. Let me give you a few examples:

- Showbiz: *Bad hair day, extreme makeover, wardrobe malfunction.*
- Military: *You buy I'll fly, bought the farm, numb nuts.*
- Sports: *Stepping up to the plate, peanut gallery, hit it out of the park.*
- Politics: *Flip-flopper, tree hugger, Kool-Aid drinker.*

The world of business seems somehow to provide the most contagious clichés and is single-handedly responsible for clogging up much of our common discourse. *To wit* (cliché):

- Thinking outside of the box.
- Win-win situation.
- Let's hit the ground running.
- Bring our "A" game.
- Value-added proposition.
- Paradigm shift.
- Low-hanging fruit.
- Giving 110 percent.
- At the end of the day.
- Seamless integration.
- Drop the ball.
- Push the envelope.
- Let's take this off-line.

- It is what it is.
- Change agent.
- The bottom line.
- The elephant in the room.
- Run it up a flagpole and see who salutes.
- Cast a wider net.
- Boots on the ground.
- Throw him under the bus.

Every one of these expressions is a whopping cliché, but we all use them. Why? Because we think of them as a short-cut to being cool, in the know, au courant. In fact, because such expressions become so overused, we can see that these expressions that are supposed to make us sound cool actually make us sound rather worn and unimaginative.

As I've mentioned, when I'm not helping students with their writing, I write marketing materials primarily for colleges and universities. When I'm writing fundraising materials, *best practice* (jargon) in the development field often dictates that the writing should be VERY SERIOUS, drawing upon words and expressions that do not sound like they come from the minds and lips of human beings. And so you'll see stuff like *utilize* for *use*, *necessitate* for *need*, *conceptualize* for *conceive*, and *dialogue* for *conversation*. Lofty/empty words rule the day: *potential, goals, transforma-tion, opportunity, empowerment, commitment, competence.* Let's avoid all those, shall we? You don't want your "last say" to come out sounding like a fundraising letter from a hospital, after all.

Nor do you want your "last say" to sound like a letter from Finkelstein, Wagner, Molinari, Kowalski & O'Brian. Legalistic language can squeeze the life out of almost any piece of writing (including legal contracts), so steer clear of anything like *aforesaid* or *prior to* or *terminate*. Always go for the simpler word, so instead of *terminate*, use *end*. Instead of *prior to*, use *before*. Always choose *if* instead of *in the event of*, *about* instead of *regarding*, *start* instead of *commence*, and *buy* instead of *purchase*. And please—under no circumstances should you ever use the expression *at this point in time* instead of *now*.

OK, that was a bit of a digression—or should we say a rant?—but we were talking about metaphors. From metaphors we made a quick hop to clichés, but let's remember that a good metaphor can be a really good thing. Just look at a piece of prose from a really good writer and you'll see how good metaphors can be. Cynthia Ozick is a great writer whose stories "The Shawl" and "Rosa," both published in the *New Yorker*, focus on a 58-year-old Holocaust survivor named Rosa, who Ozick describes as "a madwoman and a scavenger." Rosa has moved, unhappily, from New York to a hotel for the elderly in Miami. And in the first paragraph of the story, we see that setting:

The streets were a furnace, the sun an executioner. Every day without fail it blazed and blazed, so she stayed in her room and ate two bites of a hard-boiled egg in bed, with a writing board on her knees; she has taken to composing letters.

That metaphor—"the sun an executioner"—does exactly what a metaphor should do. First of all, it's arresting. It makes you sit up and take notice. Clichés (which are so often metaphors) do exactly the opposite. They are so familiar that you glaze right over them. A good metaphor is good because it is original. And it doesn't draw attention to itself with fancy words—"the sun is a guillotine"—because it is more interested in drawing attention to the concept. A good metaphor has to be consistent with the mood of the piece, or otherwise it will jump out in a very discordant, "Look at me! Look at me!" sort of way. And a metaphor that is very, very good can tell you something about a person/character's inner state of being. It creates a picture in your mind. If your metaphor doesn't do that, then don't bother with it. Again, nowhere is it written that your work must include metaphors. That said, metaphors can be very rewarding, both to the writer and to the reader. If you can create a vivid picture in your reader's mind with your metaphor, then go for it. If not, steer clear.

One other way to misuse metaphors is to mix them up in odd, ill-fitting ways—hence, the term *mixed metaphor.*

Mixed metaphors occur when you use two (or more) metaphors that simply don't go together. For instance:

- He was as sharp as a tack and as sly as a fox.
- It was a shoe box of a house with ship cabins for rooms.
- The puck shot across the ice like a bird in flight.

In at least two of these three (the first and the third), the writer mixes animal (fox, bird) images with mineral images (tack, puck). In the middle one, the writer mixes up two "mineral" metaphors (shoe box, ship cabins) that don't have any common denominator. What happens in all three cases is that too much results in too little.

BEWARE THE VAGUE PRONOUN

One of the most common ways that writers bring down the level of writing is to throw in vague pronouns. In order to understand what a vague pronoun is, you first have to understand the pronoun itself. What is a pronoun exactly? It is a word—that is, a part of speech—that takes the place of a noun or a cluster of nouns, known as a noun phrase or a noun clause. The thing to understand about a pronoun is that it's there to make it easier for the writer and the reader—not harder. The point is that you can use this little word to replace a longer word or a group of words. If pronouns had not been invented, then a piece of writing might look like this:

> The Boy Scouts of America was incorporated in 1910. William Boyce was the founder of the Boy Scouts of America. The Boy Scouts of America held the Boy Scouts of America's first annual meeting in 1911 at the White House, where President Taft addressed the Boy Scouts of America. The Boy Scouts of America named Arthur Eldred the Boy Scouts of America's First Eagle Scout in 1912.

As you might have noticed, that's a lot of "Boy Scouts of America" in a 67-word piece of text. Fortunately, the pronoun *was* invented and so the text can read like this:

> The Boy Scouts of America was incorporated in 1910. William Boyce was its founder. The Boy Scouts of America held its first annual meeting in 1911 at the White House, where President Taft addressed them. Arthur Eldred was named their first Eagle Scout in 1912.

Now the word count is 45 words—18 fewer than the version without pronouns. That means that the reader has had to do less work and appreciates that. If you track the two pieces of text, you'll see where the pronouns were used. Sometimes it doesn't work to use a pronoun because it's a bit far from the word it is replacing. Look below and you'll see what I mean:

The Boy Scouts of America was incorporated in 1910. William Boyce was its founder. It held its first annual meeting in 1911 at the White House, where President Taft addressed them. Arthur Eldred was named their first Eagle Scout in 1912.

The "It" at the beginning of the third sentence feels a bit vague because it is at a significant remove from the reference to the Boy Scouts of America. That's why the full name was used again in that position.

Specifically, vague pronouns cause an annoying problem, often referred to as "vague reference," which leads to writer and reader getting lost in a sentence. Vague reference is most likely to occur in sentences that include such words as *this*, *it*, and *which*. The writer uses such pronouns but doesn't make it clear what those pronouns refer back to. For instance:

My 60th birthday celebration was memorable. We all went for a hike, took a swim, cooked lobsters together, and that is something I will never forget.

So, in those two sentences, what does the word *that* refer to? (*That* is something I will never forget.) Is it the entirety of the experience? Is it the cooking of the lobsters? This is vague reference and it lowers the level of the writing. Better to have said:

> My 60th birthday celebration was memorable. We all went for a hike, took a swim, cooked lobsters, and, taken together, it was a day I will never forget.

Here's another example of how vague reference can throw off the reading experience:

> Mike's boss told him that he was going to be transferred.

So who is *he* in that sentence? In other words, who is going to be transferred, Mike or Mike's boss? It would be excellent to rephrase the sentence so that the reader knows exactly what is happening, along one or the other of these lines:

> "Mike, you're going to be transferred," said his boss.

or

> "I'm about to be transferred," Mike's boss told him.

Here, the vague reference is resolved by using dialogue to convey the information, but, surely, there are ways to handle this without using dialogue. I'll leave that to you.

If you can rid your writing of vague reference, you will save yourself and your readers a lot of trouble. There are many good Internet sites that are designed to help you deal with such fundamental writing problems. Do a Google search on "vague reference" and begin the work of eliminating this problem from your writing.

POINTLESS POINTS

We all have our little pet peeves. Some people can't abide cats or bananas or pay toilets or foreign call centers. I personally cannot tolerate exclamation points, unless they are following things worth exclaiming over, as in "Fire!" "Hooray!" or "Stop, thief!"

There is an epidemic of exclamation points in the air these days. I see formal essays, such as those submitted for the purposes of college admissions, which are positively strewn with exclamation points. Really! I think this has to do with the rise, over many years, of e-mail. As much as I loathe exclamation points in "real" writing, I find myself— yes, even me—ending an e-mail with "Thanks!" or "See you!" or something along those lines. Why? *Because it sounds friendly.* And who, after all, doesn't like friendly?

In a real piece of writing, however, like your "last say," exclamation points can drastically lower the level of the writing. Writers whose work is strewn with exclamation points—*It was such a proud moment! I had never been so surprised! My mother was the best friend I ever had!*—come across as desperate individuals who are trying to elevate the level of their writing with a device that they think suggests energy and élan. In fact, the opposite occurs and the eager perkiness of these punctuation marks that shout out "Love me! Love me!" only obscures the depth of feeling and meaning that is waiting to emerge. And, of course, using two exclamations at a time—!!—or three—!!!—or why not four?—!!!!—only compounds the problem exponentially. Cardinal rule: multiple exclamation points are to be used only by comic strip writers who also favor dark clouds containing such constructions as !!Ø#!! to convey a very bad day.

The Last Say: Nathalie

When she wrote her "last say," a friend whom I will call "Nathalie" was on the brink of retirement. A highly successful painter in her early 60s, Nathalie had never left her day job as a tenured professor of art, toiling for more than 30 years in the groves of academe. Now, facing the next chapter of her life, she had time for some serious reflection. An avid reader of fiction, she was developing a strong interest in writing and was eager to take on the assignment that I posed to her. Nathalie had recently lost her mother, who had been a problematic figure in her life, and I think she saw this writing challenge as an opportunity to sort out some aspects of that relationship. This is what she wrote, in its finished state:

My mother, 90, spent the last year of her life in a nursing home. Several times a week, I would drive 100 miles round-trip to see her. Having felt anger toward her for years, I was haunted by a question: Would I feel too much or too little when she died? I knew she loved me, but she had never shown it in a way I could recognize. She had always been cold, distant, and self-centered, with a default setting of doom and pessimism. But now, as my mother sat in her wheelchair and I adjusted her clothing, making sure her sweater stayed on her shoulders, I realized that I couldn't keep my hands off her. This was the physical contact I had always needed and wanted. My mother was finally letting me get close.

"How about this dusty rose color?" I said, holding up a bottle of nail polish. My mother was still very proud of her lovely hands, and the weekly ritual of painting her nails made us both happy.

The nursing home was familiar and a place of memories for both of us. My mother's mother, Grandma

Bessie, had gone there to live at the end of her life, too, and now, as I carefully applied the polish, I thought about the times we would visit Grandma Bessie and I would watch my mother sit with her when she was dying, just as I was sitting with my mother now.

"Mum," I said. "Remember Grandma's story of the baby?"

It was a story my grandmother had told my sisters and me throughout our childhood. In her ungrammatical English, she would measure out, word by word, the dramatic tale of her nighttime escape from her village in Eastern Europe. The hoodlums had come to burn the villages and Grandma Bessie's mother, my great-grandmother, made her leave that moonless night, with transport money sewn into her pocket, placing her at the end of the line of villagers that disappeared into the frozen woods. Grandma Bessie's voice cracked only when she described how she had begged and pleaded with her mother not to make her go. "Kindelich," she would say to us. "I was only 10, not much older than you are now."

"The baby?" my mother asked. The effort to retrieve the memory was visible on her face. But she soon picked up the thread of the narrative as if all intervening time had fallen away and she was a child once again, listening to the story. "You must mean Ada's baby."

Ada was Grandma Bessie's neighbor in the village.

She was too sick from just having had a baby girl to leave, so she put the baby in Grandma Bessie's arms and then ran back to the village.

My mother closed her eyes and shook her head. "Tell me. What mother does that?"

When I was a little girl, the element of trauma in my grandmother's story of upheaval and loss sailed right over my head. I cared only about what happened to the baby. To me, it was an adventure story, mystical and magical. But my mother, who had been one generation closer to this trauma, had heard the story differently. For her, it was a story of mothers and children being wrenched apart, long treks over frozen terrain, confusion, displacement, an uncertain destination, and certain death for some. When I became an adult, I understood that Grandma Bessie had been afraid to love too much. My mother had followed the same path, fearing the consequences for those who do in such an unjust and unforgiving world.

Now, sicker and weaker, having shed all her defenses—biological, mental, and emotional—my mother seemed childlike to me, and I felt a strong need to care for her in the time that remained for us. When I had finished with the nail polish, she twirled her hands in the air with a flourish to admire them and I knew there was no such thing as feeling too much.

I found this to be a most insightful and brave story, and artfully controlled as well. Sometimes it amazes me how much content can be covered in a story of 669 words. Here, three generations of family history unspool within that meager word allotment—generations of pain that give way to understanding. Then I recall that I've just read Julian Barnes's Booker Prize–winning novel, *The Sense of an Ending*, which uncannily captures the arc of several lives in a slim 162 pages. The language in Barnes's novel never feels dense (quite the opposite, actually) while the portrayal of those lives never feels less than profound. Great artists can do that—transcend the limitations of space and time—and good writers can do some semblance of that as well. I am struck, again and again, by how many "nonwriters" can produce powerful stories once they understand how stories work.

As for Nathalie's piece, I really have no idea what its ultimate application will be. I strongly doubt that she will want to have it read at her memorial service, when that time comes. She's very private—and I wouldn't be surprised if she dispensed with a memorial service altogether. At the same time, however, she was quite eager to jump into the "last say" exercise. But why not? There's really no reason why a "last say" can't be simply for you alone. If this exercise offers some measure of clarity on how you have lived your life, then why not indeed?

CHAPTER 8

Pulling It Together

B y now, you've gone through three or four or five drafts. You've felt discouraged and good and discouraged and good. Writing is like that. You're almost done now, at the point in the process where your focus is on taking care of a few remaining small issues. That said, let us also recognize that there really are no small issues when it comes to writing—or any art form, when you think about it. After all, an artist is, in a sense, borrowing your time, and we are naturally and often necessarily stingy with our time. (It's a busy world we live in.) A stage actor who forgets his lines is taking up your time. A dancer who goes in the wrong direction is not doing you any favors, either. A writer who makes mistakes, even ostensibly small ones, is distracting you and undercutting your reading experience. So we have to try to catch our mistakes, and this requires the utmost concentration and commitment to excellence. And when I say "mistakes," I mean both technical errors and lapses in judgment. Let's start with one of the latter issues first.

THE HUMAN VOICE

For a year, I wrote for *One Life to Live,* the ABC soap opera (oops, sorry—we writers were meant to say "daytime dramas"). Someone I had once worked with in the film world joined the show as a writer and she suggested I try to write for them as well. At that time, for some reason, I desperately needed some regular income (oh, yes, I remember—I had children to provide for). Luckily, I was one of about a half dozen people chosen for a soap opera writing class (oops, sorry—daytime drama) that ABC offered every few years. In my entire life, I had never watched a soap opera and my experience with dramatic writing was very limited. I did have a background with fiction, however, and, surprise of surprises, I stood out from the class so "dramatically" that I immediately got a job on *One Life.* (That job lasted a year, but that's the biz.) My secret weapon? My ear for dialogue.

Some people have an ear for dialogue, and some don't. If you're a natural mimic, you may have that gift. If you like to listen to the conversations of other people (like my wife, in restaurants, when I habitually joke that if I want her to hear me, I need to sit at an adjoining table), then that might also indicate that you have the gift. And if you do have that gift, it can come in handy. Indeed, when it comes to bringing your piece to life, there are few tools more effective than good dialogue. In fact, good dialogue will virtually leap off the page.

If you don't have an ear for dialogue, the sad news is that you're like the tennis player who doesn't have a great serve. It's awfully nice to have a great serve and it can compensate for other deficiencies, but you may never achieve that strength. The good news, however, is that you can be a terrific tennis player even if you only have an adequate serve. You just have to do everything else very, very well. And such is the case with writing. If you lack a natural ear and dialogue is not going to be your thing, then you can still be a fine writer.

If you do feel that you would like to try out some dialogue in your "last say," keep this cardinal rule in mind: dialogue is not there to provide exposition. In fact, avoid at all costs dialogue along the lines of, "Coach, I know I can do it. I've been practicing this for months. Every night, I go into my backyard and I hit the ball a hundred times. My aim and my strength are improving every day . . . yadda yadda." Dialogue is best reserved for moments like, "Coach!

Give me a chance!" That's the kind of moment that might capture a reader's attention.

As a general rule, keep your dialogue short and punchy. Most people, when they talk, do not sound like Hillary Clinton (i.e., entire paragraphs of perfectly composed prose spooling off their tongues). Keep your dialogue brief and sprightly. Use it when you want to introduce interesting new developments into the narrative. Dialogue along the order of "Hello, Danny. Looks like rain, wouldn't you say?" is just as deadly on the page as in real life. (Actually, make that more deadly. In real life, we can turn a deaf ear to such bland and bloodless exchanges. When it comes to the written page, however, we cannot easily ignore such moments.)

Another general rule? Remember that all people may be created equal, *but they are not created the same.* When you're writing dialogue, you have to become a kind of actor, inhabiting the role of whoever is speaking the dialogue. You have to realize that the minister doesn't sound like the hairdresser who doesn't sound like the pizza delivery boy. Every person has a voice that is likely to be as distinctive as his or her thumbprint. So, if you're not the kind of person who is interested in inhabiting multiple personae, you may decide to forgo dialogue altogether. That's hardly a tragedy. As I've indicated, no dialogue is better than bad dialogue.

You should also remember that even if your dialogue is

good, you run the risk of lowering the level of your writing with silly, fussy attributions. The already-cited Elmore Leonard, widely recognized as one of the supreme stylists in the field of contemporary fiction and author of books that were the basis for such films as *Get Shorty*, *Out of Sight*, and *Jackie Brown*, counseled against using any word other than *said* to carry a line of dialogue. "The line of dialogue belongs to the character," Leonard said. "The verb is the writer sticking his nose in." That means that, "'Not on my life!' Lois exploded" or "'Not on my life!' Lois interjected" or "'Not on my life!' Lois roared" are all less desirable than "'Not on my life!' Lois said." Those attributions are meant to sort of disappear, and when Lois is roaring or interjecting, the opposite happens. And, again, I urge you to avoid adding adverbs when you are attributing a line of dialogue. "'Not on my life!' Lois said sternly" or "'Not on my life!' Lois said furiously" are actually inferior to the pure, simple, "'Not on my life!' Lois said."

DON'T QUOTE ME

Want to know what's sure to bring down the level of your "last say" in record time, rendering it both impersonal and banal? The quotation from some famous person that you have sourced in Bartlett's or on some Internet quotations site. Consider such as these:

- "Believe that life is worth living and your belief will help create the fact."—William James
- "All life is an experiment. The more experiments you make the better."—Ralph Waldo Emerson
- "Only a life lived for others is a life worthwhile." —Albert Einstein

Three thoughts from three great thinkers and they all have a certain intrinsic merit, but do us a favor and let James, Emerson, and Einstein put those thoughts into *their* "last says," OK? These kinds of quotations feel dreary enough when you happen to be sitting at your child's college graduation and some big donor who helped build the new student union is asked to give the commencement address. But in *your* "last say"? I think not. Let's reserve your "last say" for your very own thoughts, instead of something that you have so transparently borrowed from the public domain.

CRITICAL FEEDBACK

I'd like to take a short detour in this chapter from our discussion of various odds and ends to focus, for a moment, on the issue of getting critical readings of your work. I've alluded to this before, but it's worth another go-round, as this process can be rewarding and painful—at the same time, in equal measure.

If you're not a person who is particularly used to expressing yourself in words, then the prospect of writing your "last say" and then showing it to people and getting back their opinions could very well be . . . well, *terrifying* is an apt word. The act of writing is very exposed, very naked, and when you combine being naked with not being young, as most of us reading this are (not), then it doesn't paint a pretty picture. When you write something, it's important to keep in mind how other people will read it or hear it. Writing is not a one-way street. Well, if you immediately stash what you wrote in your back closet, beneath the itchy red cardigan you never wear, then perhaps it is. But if you write it for sharing, which is mostly the intent of this exercise, the potential for some hurt and disappointment is there.

Hurt and disappointment? you say tremulously. (Ha! Gotcha! Clumsy adverb on the attribution.)

Yes, it hurts to write something and to discover that others are not getting it. It's frustrating and mystifying and altogether a pain. But that's the nature of the beast. Keep in mind that some of the greatest books of all time got their share of lousy reviews. To wit, these extraordinary novels—all cited on *Time* magazine's list of the 100 best English-language novels ever:

- *Lolita* by Vladimir Nabokov. "There are two equally serious reasons why it isn't worth any adult reader's attention. The first is that it is dull, dull, dull in a pretentious, florid and archly fatuous fashion. The second is that it is repulsive." —Orville Prescott, *New York Times*, 1958

- *Catch-22* by Joseph Heller. "The book is an emotional hodgepodge; no mood is sustained long enough to register for more than a chapter." —Richard G. Stern, *New York Times Book Review*, 1961

- *The Great Gatsby* by F. Scott Fitzgerald. ". . . an absurd story, whether considered as romance, melodrama, or plain record of New York high life." —L. P. Hartley, *Saturday Review*, 1925

This one is not on the list, as it's French, but I love it:

- *Madame Bovary* by Gustave Flaubert. "Monsieur Flaubert is not a writer." —*Le Figaro*, 1857

Needless to say, the Messrs. Nabokov, Heller, Fitzgerald, and Flaubert have gone on to immortality, while their reviewers have gone the way of all flesh.

Please understand that it is a good thing to get readings on your piece, but it's also a good thing to go into this "review" process with some understanding of how it works.

Here are a few points to keep in mind as you gather and assess these readings:

- *Know that all critical feedback is not created equal.* Some readers are more sensitive to the written word than others. Some are more emotionally available than others. Some are smarter than others. If you feel that the feedback you are getting is not especially valuable, then there's no need to take it to heart.

- *Listen—don't defend.* No need to get all hot and bothered by a little criticism—assuming that it is constructive criticism. If someone reads something you wrote and he or she says, "Hey, Jack, this stinks," well, that may be a time to get hot and bothered. But most people are not looking to be aggressive when they're asked to read something. In fact, for the layperson, giving feedback can be as anxiety-producing as receiving feedback.

- *Be alert to common themes.* If you're finding some consistency to the feedback you're receiving— *Confusing; I didn't get it; It felt a little slow*—then maybe you'd best be paying some attention. The average reader will very likely speak in generalities and may not have anything specifically constructive to say, but it's not the reader's job to fix flaws. That's the job of the writer.

- *Tell yourself it can be fixed.* Most things can be. If your reader feels that your piece is too confusing, you may have to alter the structure. If people aren't relating to the characters, you'll have to examine the actions of those characters or their language or the point of view to try to figure out what's wrong. If The Point of your essay isn't coming across, then you may have to state your point more explicitly . . . or perhaps less explicitly. Examine your piece from all different angles to see whether you've missed something, but, whatever you do, don't despair—the essay may only require a little extra investment of energy to get it right.

- *Put it down.* You don't want to worry a piece to death, robbing it of its life force with too much nattering about. Put your piece out there for readings—and then put it down when you feel you've had enough.

It's also important to point out that what you've written in your "last say" may very well touch on feelings and push emotional buttons in the lives of those around you (who are very likely to be the people you've given this to for readings). Don't expect something neutral if you're treading on territory that has to do with other people.

If you choose to read your drafts to someone else, just know that getting more feedback than you know what to do with at the first-draft stage can be counterproductive. At this early stage, you might simply designate just one person as your "trusted reader." Ideally, this is a person who radiates an interest and respect in things like books, films, and other forms of the written word. Many of us tend to know at least a few such people in our worlds. Now that person could well be your spouse, but spouses, as I don't have to tell you, are not exactly neutral. I remember once writing a short story that had to do with my mother-in-law, who lived with us for five years after she was diagnosed with Alzheimer's disease. The story touched on the frustration and sometimes anger that was engendered by living with this situation. My wife, at that time also a working writer, was somebody I always turned to for feedback but, in this instance, when her feedback was quite negative, I remember feeling that her negativity might have had more to do with the nerves I had touched than with the story itself. In other words, spouses can be too close to provide the kind of feedback you're looking for, and they may focus on feelings and attitudes that are expressed—*What do you mean you never liked Uncle Mike? What do you mean our first apartment was a dump?*—instead of on the writing itself.

COMMON MISTAKES

There's a big difference between what you're striving to do with your "last say" and what my high school students are doing with their application essays. While there is a strong analogous relationship in the sense that both are examples of life review, the high schoolers are tasked with creating something that is as error-free as possible. If they use "who" and "whom" incorrectly, some counselor at Yale or Washington University or UCLA might think less of them. So we can't risk that and we pore over the work to make sure it is as technically perfect as we can make it. You, on the other hand, are not going to be judged that way. If your "last say" has some technical errors, so be it. However, do keep in mind that one of your goals here is to create a keepsake, and if something is going to live on, in any sense, isn't it much nicer if it does so without silly mistakes?

In the interest of helping you to create a clean piece of writing, I just want to do a quick roundup of some of the technical errors that I find to be the most common—and the most nettlesome. Here we go:

- **It's/Its.** It's amazing how far in life one can go without understanding the difference between these two usages. I see this mistake popping up all over the place all of the time. So in order to promote better writing across the board, let me try to quickly clear this one up. *It's* is a contraction of *it is.* (*It's raining*). *Its* is a possessive—that is, the thing that belongs to *it.* (*Hollywood has lost its glamour.*) One quick and easy way to get a handle on this is to substitute *his* (or *her*) for *its.* If that doesn't work, then *it's* probably will. Get it?

- **Their/there.** This one is just too easy to not get it right. *There* is a noun meaning "a place, position, or point" or an adverb meaning "in, at, or toward that place," while *their* is a possessive meaning "belonging to them."

- **Lose/loose.** This little demon is also easy to clear up. You *lose* at Scrabble. You carry *loose* change in your pocket. The verb that sounds like *ooze* is *lose.* The word that has a hissy sound that rhymes with *goose* is *loose.*

- **Affect/effect.** There are actually four distinct meanings surrounding these two words. With *affect*, when the accent is on the final syllable (a-FECT), you have a verb meaning "to have an influence on." *Alcohol will affect your performance.* A second meaning of *affect*, when the accent is on the first syllable (AFF-ect), is much less frequently encountered. This term, meaning "emotion," is mostly used by psychologists, as in *The patient had little visible affect.* These two words should not be confused with the commonly used noun *effect*, as in *The effect of the drug on Jim's condition was powerful.* Less commonly, *effect* is used as a verb meaning "to create," as in *Peace activists try to effect change in many ways.* In general, however, it will serve you well to remember that *affect* is most often used as a verb while *effect* is most often used as a noun, as in "When you *affect* a situation, your actions have an *effect.*"

- **A lot.** This expression, which means "a great deal or a great amount," is *always* spelled as two words—*a lot.* There is no such word as *alot.* Just as you would never write "alittle," so should you never write "alot."

- **I/me/myself.** People often trip themselves up on the use of this pronoun, so, again, let me try to quickly clear things up for you. *I* is always used as a subject. You would say, for instance, *I am going to the library.* If you had a friend with you, you would say, *Jill and I are going to the library. I* is never used as an object. *He passed the menus to Bill and I* is incorrect. *He passed the menus to Bill and me* is correct. A quick way to test when there's more than one object, one of which is *I,* is to take out the other object. So if you change *He passed the menus to Bill and I* to *He passed the menus to I*, you'll probably hear the mistake there, yes?

- **Who/Whom.** Here's another one that's a complete mystery for many people. *Whom* is essentially a dying word. You'll rarely hear it spoken, but it's still used occasionally in formal writing. The distinction between *who* and *whom* is basically simple. *Who* is the subject form of the pronoun, as in *Who gave you those flowers? Whom* is the object form, as in *Jen's mother was so surprised when Jen walked in with a bouquet of flowers that she forgot to whom she was talking on the telephone.* Of course, in this day and age, if you were to rewrite that sentence as *Jen's mother was so surprised when Jen walked in with a bouquet of flowers that she forgot who she was talking to on the telephone*, it would be considered totally correct and, in fact, considerably less stiff and stuffy. Perhaps the only instance in which you'll still see *whom* used regularly is in the salutation of a business letter that begins *To whom this may concern.* To stop worrying about *whom*, try to rewrite your sentences so that you don't need it—as with the example cited above of Jen's mom forgetting who she was talking to on the phone.

- **Good/well.** Another frequently confused pair. *Good* is an adjective; *well* is an adverb. *He did well on the test* is correct. *This ice cream tastes good* is also correct, as compared to *This ice cream tastes well.* Of course, because common usage changes the standards of correctness, people say, *I feel good* and *I feel well* interchangeably without raising any eyebrows.

- **Then/than.** When comparing one thing with another, use *than. Max is older than Fred.* If you're talking about time, use *then. First, I'll put on the kettle, and then we'll sit down and talk.*

- **No one.** *No one* is always written as two words. There is no such word as *noone.*

- **Unique.** Here's a little one that personally makes me crazy, so bear with me on my personal stamp-it-out crusade. *Unique* means "having no like or equal." It is absolute. *The* Mona Lisa *is a unique work of art.* You wouldn't say, *The* Mona Lisa *is the most unique work of art* or *a more unique work of art* or *a less unique work of art.* You don't apply qualifiers of "more" or "less" to *unique*—as I say, it is absolute.

There are a lot more ways you can slip up—and it won't be the end of the world—but this could be a good start on reining in those errors.

ISSUES NOT TO WORRY ABOUT

We writers of a certain age were taught certain rules way back when that we can now blessedly ignore. The reason I'm even bringing this up is to liberate you and make sure that you're not getting hung up on those silly rules when what you really want to do is have some free expression in your pieces. For instance, we all learned, when we were kids, that you're not supposed to start a sentence with *but* or *and*, right? Well, children, that was not such a good rule. You can certainly start a sentence with *But* or *And*—just not too frequently. In fact, there are times when it makes good sense to start a sentence with a conjunction. Consider this:

> Estelle and Michael met on an online site for those over 50. Neither one of them ever thought that he or she would wind up there; it felt kind of desperate to them. But it worked so much better than they ever thought it would. The anonymity allowed them to experiment without fear of exposure, and it was exciting.

Is that third sentence wrong because it starts with *but*? Not at all. There you have an example of starting a sentence with a conjunction in a way that is actually thought out and chosen for style. Estelle and Michael had been hesitant about using an online dating service. But it worked for them. And the way that the *but* is placed at the beginning of that sentence suggests, to my ear at least, a kind of surprise.

Think back to the time when we were grade school kids. Native Americans were called Indians, Columbus was considered to be a great guy (at least, Ferdinand and Isabella thought so), and you *never, ever* ended a sentence with a preposition. So it's not unusual for me to see my baby boomer writers turning out sentences like this:

Today, my piano teacher focused on the pedals and explained the purpose for which they were designed.

Now, I would regard that as a rather convoluted, stiff, and awkward construction. To me, it would have been easier to simply write:

Today, my piano teacher focused on the pedals and explained what they are used for.

Oh, but wait. That's ending a sentence on a dreaded preposition. Can't do that!

Now hear this, folks: there is nothing wrong with ending a sentence on a preposition. The good, clean writing to which you should be aspiring is really about achieving a natural feeling and rhythm and that means relaxing old rules. There is a wonderfully astringent quote from Winston Churchill that pretty much puts an end to this particular tempest in a teapot. When Churchill was asked what he thought of ending a sentence with a preposition, he stoutly declared the following: "This is the sort of English up with which I shall not put."

Ah. So many silly rules getting in the way of so much good, challenging, expansive writing to be done. Put the rules down and focus instead on telling your story. Here's a writer who did just that.

The Last Say: Barbara

Throughout this book, I've used the term *life review* with regard to these essays, and I particularly feel the aptness of that phrase when I look back on my work with Barbara.

Barbara, who is roughly my age, lives in the country, as I do, but she is a much more recent transplant from New York City and one has the impression that she never goes out of the house without her earrings on. She is impeccably groomed, an outstanding and meticulous hostess, and her home would make Martha Stewart drool. That said, Barbara has had a tough life that has included divorce, raising a child pretty much on her own, dealing with ongoing severe musculoskeletal issues that stem from a very bad accident she had as a young woman, as well as a history of eating disorders.

Talk about Conflict.

The way that Barbara has dealt with all that is by living an examined life and, for her, this "last say" exercise was yet another way to gain insight into what she had gone through and was continuing to go through. And so she jumped at the chance to review her life through a discipline she had not made much use of before: writing.

Barbara's answers to my exploratory questions were unusually frank and, again, full of Conflict. There was one question-and-answer combination, however, that jumped out at me. In response to the question, "Have I ever changed the course of someone else's life?" Barbara said, "I like to think so. I certainly made an impact on a young woman I met in rehab who came to live with us for a time while she continued in an outpatient program in New York City."

To me, that was an "Aha!" moment, because if there was one thing I recognized about Barbara, who I had known for some time, it was that she was a person who valued relationships with other people. She was warm, she liked to entertain, she had a social conscience that led her to go beyond what many others might do, such as taking a deploying soldier's dog for a year, and these things suggested to me that somewhere in her "last say" she should reflect that value of doing for others and *connecting* with others.

Also, as I have said, I really like essays that are layered. So instead of an essay that is exclusively about coping with an eating disorder—which can certainly be a huge challenge in a person's life and accordingly merits real attention—you can come to that subject through another door.

Barbara agreed. Here is what she came up with for her "last say," for which she had a clever and ironic title that you'll understand when you come to the end:

The ι η π Sorority

They walked down East 32nd Street arm in arm on a Monday morning in late October. It was warm, but the damp red and orange leaves piled up on the sewer grate reminded her that the early weeks of autumn had passed her by. She felt lost in the city she had known all her life. In spite of this, she had promised the parents of the girl who walked beside her that she would personally take their daughter to her destination that morning.

The two women had only met eight short weeks earlier and now clung to each other like life preservers. They were an odd pair; she fifty, the other nineteen; one soon to be retired, the other still in college; a sophisticated woman of New York and an immature girl from the Midwest. What they shared were their emaciated frames, sallow faces, sadness, and lack of hunger, both for food and for life.

They first noticed each other across a crowded room of females, mostly girls and young women who had the recognizable look of anorexia and who more than likely had other hidden eating disorder secrets. As the saying goes, "it takes one to know one," but she did not recognize herself among those in the room. She didn't understand how these girls came to be there. They were responsible, smart, funny, attractive, and talented. They were enrolled at Brown, Dartmouth, Skidmore, and Michigan. They had been cheerleaders, pianists, harpists, and athletes. Some were still in high school. What had happened in these girls' lives that landed them in a clinic for eating disorders? And were they not wondering the same about her?

Over the next weeks, she listened and observed as people spoke and cried, play acted and painted, and while the specifics of their stories were different than her own journey, she found familiarity in the thoughts and beliefs. There began to be comfort in hearing the words; words she rarely uttered aloud but ones that played over and over in her head. Hers came from the imaginary two-inch devil that sat on her right shoulder jabbing her with its pitchfork as it ridiculed and told her she was disgusting and of no worth to anyone. They were the words that resulted in her total isolation, unable to think about anything but food, abstaining from it or eating it, but, most importantly, controlling it. It had happened fast, the spiral out of control. Spurred on by family members, she had agreed to seek help, soon learning that it would require intensive inpatient rehabilitation.

The work was hard and painful but made easier by the understanding and camaraderie between the patients. They all learned to rely on each other, committed to successfully conquering their demons. The inexplicable life they shared bonded them. It was an exclusive and unique club, the "I Ate a Pie" ($\iota\ \eta\ \pi$) Sorority. To join, one must have experienced the depths of despair and the convoluted thinking emblematic of its members.

As the two sorority sisters turned into the nondescript, midcentury office building, they gave each other a squeeze and a smile. No words were said. Having been released just days before, they were frightened yet secure in the knowledge that they would travel the next road together. Arm in arm, they crossed the threshold into the rest of their lives, the outpatient program.

Do you see what I mean when I tell you that people who do not think of themselves as writers can create truly powerful pieces of writing? And why, after all, should writing belong only to writers when so many people have the capacity to be really good at it, even if it's only for one prescribed assignment?

Barbara is a very good natural writer, and so her writing choices were inventive and solid. A while back, we were talking about point of view and I said that most of you would probably wind up writing your pieces in the first person. There is no rule, however, that says you have to do that and, in any case, writing is all about breaking the rules (which is easier to do once you understand the form you're working in). Barbara chose to use a third-person perspective when telling her story and I think you'll agree that her decision made perfect sense. It captures, in a kind of hauntingly detached way, the feeling she had about that period in her life when she felt utterly distanced from herself and others, clinging to the "life preserver" of another human being who understood what she was going through when so many others could not.

As a "last say," it works beautifully. It opens a window into a private side of Barbara and, in doing so, provides a great gift to her family and friends. It also passes down an ethical value, specifically that there is sustenance to be found in making connections with other people. In both respects, Barbara's "last say" becomes a testament that makes perfect sense for her.

CHAPTER 9

Go Forth (And One Last Say)

As much as this book is about life review, it's just as much about writing, which is really a very complicated thing. After spending a lifetime writing, I can only say that it has been the source of my greatest frustrations and my peak moments of exhilaration. Those feelings have even coexisted, side by side, in very strange ways.

Writing allows you to endlessly explore the world and yourself and yourself in the world, and naturally that can be exciting and exhausting at the same time. Writing takes you to the darkest places, but hopefully you will make that journey in a trim craft that you have created out of sheer will and discipline. All of the discipline and will in the world, however, won't preclude disappointment and difficulties at the end. As William Faulkner once said, "The work never matches the dream of perfection the artist has to start with."

But, again, let us not forget the pleasure and even joy that can come out of the act of writing. I often see both my high school and adult writers experiencing such sensations. To them, there is something miraculous in the way that a solid narrative structure can lead them to places they could never have imagined they would visit. They shock themselves with the power of their expression and the elegance of their phrases. And, as I've said before, the vast majority of the people I work with do not identify themselves as writers. (Ironically, the ones who do often have the most difficulty with the process.)

I don't know what the writers of these "last says" will ultimately do with them. Thank God, none have left us yet, so I cannot report that their "last says" have been read at their memorial services. I suspect many will keep these writings in drawers for other people to find one day—or not. And that's all well and good. The experience has left them with insight into themselves and has fostered a sense of community with their fellow writers with whom they have shared this experience. Isn't that enough?

The Last Say: **Tamar** When I was working on this book, I told my writer friend Tamar all about what I was doing and she was intrigued. Tamar and I first met in that soap opera writing class I mentioned some pages ago. (Oops! Daytime drama!)

Neither of us had ever written a stitch of daytime drama before we joined this class and we really didn't know *The Guiding Light* from *The Young and the Restless*. All we knew was that the money was good—and that we needed money. Alas, neither of us lasted more than a year in that strange and tumultuous subculture, but, even though our intersection was brief, we have managed to maintain a long-distance friendship for close to 25 years.

Tamar is a writer of fiction, nonfiction, and drama. She comes from a family of writers, several generations' worth, some quite well known. Tamar has not had an easy life as a writer. Too often, she has been on the cusp of wider recognition, and has had to deal with many disappointments and financial struggles. Over the years, to support her writing, she has worked quite a bit as a private investigator and so she has witnessed a lot of Conflict. She has written about some of that and she has also done many of the same sorts of keeping-afloat activities that I and many other writers engage in: marketing, public relations, and all that stuff. When I told Tamar about my book and described the way I had been working with adult writers, she sensed that there might also be an opportunity for her to do such work up in Vermont, where she lives. I told Tamar, however, that if she wanted to do this work, she would first have to do a "last say" of her own and I would work with her, so that she would understand the process and then be ready to go and work with others.

Tamar was eager to try this and so she did the exercise with the exploratory questions. I was a bit surprised when I received them. They felt quite guarded and nothing immediately jumped out at me as a potential "last say." There were two themes, however, that reappeared in many of her answers. One had to do with the great difficulty and stress she encountered around her writing. The other had to do with the pleasure she took in some of life's most elemental experiences: parenting, for instance, and being in nature, especially at her beloved Maine coast. I suggested she try to write something that juxtaposed those two themes and she wrote the following essay, which I think makes for instructive reading for anyone who is about to sit down to a blank page.

I was in Maine working on the rewrite of a play. I was on the fourth, fifth, or sixth draft. I had lost count. I had also lost the thread. What was I writing about? And why? The story I wanted to tell, once a vivid oil painting in my mind, had become an intangible pale watercolor, barely recognizable to me. Too much input from interested parties; directors, producers, people who claimed to love the story but had many opinions about what it should be. The familiar strain of being at the desk, uninspired, wondering why I shouldn't just walk away and do something useful, productive, more enjoyable . . . all of it sat like a lump of sour milk churning in my gut. I closed the laptop and stood up.

Ennui swept over me. I lay down on the bed, wishing I were a person who could nap, who could close her eyes and drift off and forget about the nonsense of writing. I heard the sound of the woodpecker pounding away at the same tree he had been pounding on all summer long. Impressed with his fortitude, I stood up and returned to my desk, but it only took seconds to recognize the fruitlessness of that act. I grabbed a sweater, headed out the door, and walked to the edge of the lawn, down a set of wooden stairs, and onto the rocky shore of my beloved Maine coast.

The tides in Maine are long, and the morning mist covering the low tide just coming in was so dense that I could barely see the water. Seagulls circled above and moved off at the crunching of my steps over the shells and seaweed that blanketed the mud. I was mad. Pointless rumblings ran through my mind. *If I had a bigger name no one would have questioned my first draft. The fact that I didn't was my fault.* Though I had been writing all my life, and found comfort and a sense of purpose from little else, I often stopped writing for extended periods of time. When I asked myself why, which I did on a regular basis, a cacophony, posing as words, convinced me to jump away and abandon not only the work, but opportunities that arose from the work. Did the reasons I gave myself even matter? What good came of analyzing? Wasn't it enough to note that *not writing* made me feel terrible? Ach! Thinking about it made me more fatigued. I hated the whole business. Why was I even writing a play?

I strolled out to a large rock and climbed on top of it. The tide was just beginning to slowly seep back to shore. As I sat watching the sea move inch by inch toward land, I became aware that I was hunched over and my breathing was shallow. I sat up straight, closed my eyes, took a deep breath, and let the sea air wash through me. Slowly, I picked my head up and looked toward the horizon. I had been coming to this place for forty years and loved it. The pristine northern beauty of the coves bordered on all sides by pine trees and the long tides that uncovered tidal pools of sea life always put me at ease. I took another deep breath, listening to the sea lap its way closer and closer to the rock where I sat. Just as I was about to climb off the rock and head back to shore before the water became too deep, the sun peeked through the mist and lit up the cove. I closed my eyes, basking in the sun. As I did, I realized that my dark thoughts and mood had lifted. Like magic, the frustrating story of failure had vanished.

I climbed off the rock and took a circuitous route back to the house, strolling with the tide that very slowly followed me to shore. I got to the stairs leading to the lawn and turned to look back at the water. The seagulls squawked to one another and the sun sparkled across the cove. It was hard to leave. I sat down on the steps as the sea completed its tide, covering the shore. A thought occurred to me about a character in the play and a line she needed to say. I became lost in the play, thinking about how that one line would solidify the scene I was working on, and that led to another idea about how to end the act. I was excited, stood up and moved quickly up the stairs, anxious to get to work. Entering the house I was full of energy and anticipation. I made a cup of tea, and went upstairs. I put my tea down on the windowsill next to my desk and opened my computer. I pulled out my chair and sat down. The woodpecker was still working away on his tree. I toasted him and took a sip of tea. I began outlining the scene I had imagined on the beach. I smiled thinking about how the negative thoughts were still there, they always were, yammering away at one another all the time, vying for my attention. But at this moment, they no longer mattered. Nothing mattered but the work. I was writing.

I looked back at the cove and nodded. How well it had reminded me that the work doesn't come from the incessant chatter of what success is or isn't. It comes from the quiet, from the inside.

When I read this piece, I felt quite moved by it. I identified with the struggles that come with writing. I also identified with the release and calm that comes from connecting to everyday things in the world around us, although, in the spirit of full disclosure, I must admit that it has taken me many years to allow myself to experience those more positive feelings. First, I had to work through some private personal traps that writing represented for me. That wasn't easy.

Tamar's piece and all of the other pieces in this book, and in subsequent work I have done with the adults who collaborated with me, made me think about Socrates's famous quote: *The unexamined life is not worth living.* I believe that the urge to examine life lies at the heart of writing. Engaging in this kind of close examination is enormously difficult—but can be enormously rewarding. All these folks I have worked with who have never done this kind of work before came away from the experience with a feeling of fulfillment. They had examined their lives and that very examination wound up feeling like a validation of who they are. They had done something brave and that always feels good. And they had created a gift for others, and that feels good as well. I also believe that the fact that they were dealing with a canvas of workable size—500 to 1,000 words—allowed these writers to take on and realize their goals. To write 500 to 1,000 words of quality prose is not an easy task for anyone, but, on the other hand, it's not *Moby-Dick*.

Take on this challenge and I believe you will find that this is just the right work to be doing at this time of life. So try it. Be brave, be open, go forward, and enjoy.

ACKNOWLEDGMENTS

The creation of *Having the Last Say* was truly a collaborative effort. I would like to thank my agent, Reiko Davis, for her enthusiasm and expertise and Miriam Altshuler for connecting me with her. Joanna Ng, my editor, has been consistently insightful and worth listening to. Thank you to my trusting writers who engaged in this process with me: Tamar Cole, Janina Deppe, Laurie Kaplowitz, Steve Kerner, Lydia Kukoff, Barbara Lax, Anne Rosen, Alice Swersey, Rachel Weisman, and Dan Wise. And, always, loving thanks to my wife and fellow traveler, Karen Levine.

INDEX

ALSO BY ALAN GELB

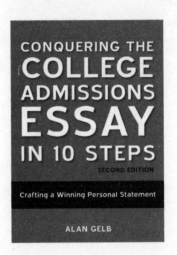

The bestselling book that has enabled thousands to turn
a daunting writing assignment into an opportunity to shine

"This indispensable resource clearly outlines the qualities and tech-
niques that make for superb personal statements."

—SUE WASIOLEK, DEAN OF STUDENTS AT DUKE UNIVERSITY
AND CO-AUTHOR OF *Getting the Best Out of College*

Visit http://conquerthecollegeessay.com for more information.